Population Politics in Twentieth-Century Europe

Historical Connections
Series editors
Tom Scott, University of Liverpool
Geoffrey Crossick, University of Essex
John Davis, University of Connecticut
Joanna Innes, Somerville College, University of Oxford

Titles in the series

Population Politics in Twentieth-Century Europe

Fascist dictatorships and liberal democracies

Maria Sophia Quine

ROUTLEDGE

London and New York

To my Θείτσα, with love and gratitude

First published 1996
by Routledge
11 New Fetter Lane, London EC4P 4EE

Simultaneously published in the USA and Canada
by Routledge
29 West 35th Street, New York, NY 10001

Phototypeset in Times by Intype, London
Printed and bound in Great Britain by
Clays Ltd, St Ives plc

British Library Cataloguing in Publication Data
A catalogue record for this book is available from the British Library

Library of Congress Cataloguing in Publication Data
Quine, Maria Sophia.
    Population politics in twentieth-century Europe : fascist
    dictatorships and liberal democracies / Maria Sophia Quine.
    p.   cm. – (Historical connections)
    Includes bibliographical references and index.
    1. Italy – Population policy.   2. France – Population policy.
    3. Germany – Population policy.   I. Series.
    HB3599.Q46   1996
    363.9′0945–dc20   95–8636

ISBN 0–415–08069–X

Contents

Series editors' preface

Historical Connections is a series of short books on important historical topics and debates, written primarily for those studying and teaching history. The books will offer original and challenging works of synthesis that will make new themes accessible, or old themes accessible in new ways, build bridges between different chronological periods and different historical debates, and encourage comparative discussion in history.

If the study of history is to remain exciting and creative, then the tendency to fragmentation must be resisted. The inflexibility of older assumptions about the relationship between economic, social, cultural and political history has been exposed by recent historical writing, but the impression has sometimes been left that history is little more than a chapter of accidents. This series will insist on the importance of processes of historical change, and it will explore the connections within history: connections between different layers and forms of historical experience, as well as connections that resist the fragmentary consequences of new forms of specialism in historical research.

Historical Connections will put the search for these connections back at the top of the agenda by exploring new ways of uniting the different strands of historical experience, and by affirming the importance of studying change and movement in history.

Geoffrey Crossick
John Davis
Joanna Innes
Tom Scott

Acknowledgements

I would like to thank my students for inspiring me to choose this topic. Their interest in the great men, great wars and great moments in history showed me the shortcomings of traditional A-level and undergraduate syllabi. That women and babies, birthing and rearing, sex and reproduction got so many statesmen and scientists hot and bothered has not yet received much attention in conventional curricula. One of the editors of this series, John Davis, has lent his friendship and support for a number of years now. During a difficult postgraduate apprenticeship, he often acted as a surrogate supervisor by parenting a doctoral thesis that might otherwise never have been completed. I am deeply grateful to him for that and for his encouragement to write this short book. The chapter on Germany benefited enormously from a reading by Richard J. Evans, who kindly provided detailed comments. I am indebted to Claire L'Enfant at Routledge for her patience. Infinite thanks are also due to Stephen Church. He carefully read the manuscript and graciously tolerated my moods.

Introduction

Fears of 'over-population' and 'depopulation' in the nineteenth century

For much of the eighteenth century, statesmen saw population growth as a precondition for economic progress. The mercantilist belief that an abundance of cheap labour was a source of national wealth and security encouraged governments to adopt pronatalist policies. The prevailing view was that a plentiful supply of workers stimulated manufactures, generated demand for goods and promoted trade. And states needed soldiers and sailors to man navies and armies for war. Physiocrats and *philosophes* alike presumed that an expanding population created the commercial prosperity and industrial productivity on which people's health and happiness depended. By the eve of the nineteenth century, however, attitudes towards demographic increment had changed dramatically. An unprecedented rise in fertility after 1750 provoked widespread alarm over the threat of over-population. Renowned thinkers like Montesquieu, Benjamin Franklin, James Stewart, Arthur Young and Joseph Townsend all feared that a rapid increase in the birthrate would lower standards of living. This anxiety also haunted the mind of T. R. Malthus, who published his completed *Essay on the Principle of Population* in 1803. A mathematician by training, Malthus was one of the founders of demography, a new science based on the collection of vital statistics whose aim was to uncover population trends and to predict their outcome. Contributing to contemporary debates in political economy, Malthus argued that excessive population growth impoverished nations.

Malthus (1766–1834) lived through the beginnings of the process of economic and social change which transformed Britain from a largely agrarian society into the first industrialized nation. He witnessed the early stages of industrialization when England underwent an 'agricultural revolution' characterized by the spread of improved farming and grazing techniques. The enclosure of wastelands and improved husbandry increased the productivity of land and labour. The rise of a money economy and the commercialization of agriculture caused a phenomenal growth in food supply which was accompanied by a boom in births. England's population went from 5.576 million to 8.664 million in the years from 1741 to 1801 (McLaren 1984: 9). Although Malthus was unaware of the extent of the population explosion which took place in the second half of the eighteenth century, he believed that the labouring poor were reproducing at a rate which far exceeded the country's ability to sustain them. The economic resources of even a wealthy nation like England, which produced food and commodities in abundance, did not increase quickly enough and were not distributed equitably enough to support a surplus population. In his *Essay*, Malthus departed from such predecessors as Adam Smith and David Hume when he asserted that the inherent inequalities of the new market system dictated that labour be undervalued and some be kept in poverty, so no humble working man could afford to feed a large family on a slim wage packet. Therefore, a steadily rising population resulted in 'a want of the means of subsistence' which 'impeded the progress of mankind towards happiness' (Malthus 1982: 5 and 106).

Malthus based this pessimistic belief in the peril of over-population on the premise that 'there was no bound' to the prolific nature of human beings. He presumed that individuals had no innate ability to contain their biologically ordained sexual drive and reproductive urges. 'Man', he believed, was a creature of the flesh ruled by an irremediable instinct to reproduce the species. Unless war, epidemic or famine occurred, people would procreate so copiously that they would endanger first their livelihood and then their own survival. To avoid catastrophe, population, he argued, 'must always be kept down to the level of the means of subsistence' (Malthus 1982: 2 and 5–6). He identified the existence of certain 'preventive checks' on the 'reckless over-breeding' which created widespread poverty and misery among the 'lower orders of society, which in any nation form the most numerous class' (Malthus 1982: 126). Chief among these was a distinct European pattern of late marriage which he welcomed as an ideal method of limiting the size of families. He posited that without a constraint like the postponement of marriage a population would multiply in constant geometric proportions, thereby doubling itself every twenty-five years. Malthus also postulated that economic resources always increased in quantity only at a much slower arithmetic rate. Thus, the steady growth in the amount of food produced could never keep pace with ever escalating demographic demand.

A crisis of over-population would inevitably occur after a sustained rise in the birthrate. Malthus presented his gloomy prediction as an absolute 'principle of population' and even an iron 'law of nature' which destined 'man' to suffer from an unavoidable disequilibrium between food and population (Malthus 1982: 151).

Malthus had some faith in the ability of people to control their sexual behaviour if not their biological nature. Society should not, he upheld, enable individuals to have as many children as they pleased and thereby 'multiply too fast' (Malthus 1982: 152). The inevitable trend towards over-population could only be reversed if more people could be convinced to show some prudential control over natural procreative urges which caused 'conjugal love' to sink into 'mere animal desire' (Malthus 1982: 156). Malthus championed the idea that human beings' innate search for 'gratification' to the point of 'repletion' should be tempered by reason and morality. He became the apostle of a new creed which asked followers to recognize the 'evils' of unbridled sexual desires and to 'civilize' themselves by using 'moral restraint' to contain their passions (Malthus 1982: 153–4). As his detractors often pointed out, Malthus was a Protestant parson whose religious convictions influenced his scientific approach to the apparent problem of reckless overbreeding. Though an advocate of birth control, he remained opposed to abortion, as well as to all forms of contraception. While he believed that sex was a pleasure conceived by the 'Creator' as an encouragement for human beings to replenish themselves plentifully, he also argued that 'excessive' physical love, even within marriage, was sinful. The indulgence of every sexual whim, however natural, made men indolent and lethargic, less concerned to increase the means of subsistence by their industry and labour (Malthus 1982: 156–7). Despite, or perhaps because of, his moralizing bent, Malthus' disciples abounded in the early nineteenth century.

Many agreed with the notion that a prudent limitation of births was a prerequisite for continued material and spiritual progress. Belief in the instinctual drive of human beings to reproduce too plentifully and the fatal tendency of the population to outgrow the means of subsistence became the official orthodoxy. In the first edition of *The Origin of Species* which appeared in 1859, Charles Darwin predicated his discovery of the process of 'natural selection' on Malthus' definition of the physiology and sexuality of human beings. He wrote that a 'struggle for existence inevitably follows from the high rate at which all organic beings tend to increase'. Darwin, therefore, took Malthus' 'principle of population' to be the very mechanism which caused evolutionary change. As populations tend to increase at a 'geometric' rate, he wrote, the pressures brought about by this growth are so great that 'more individuals are produced than can possibly survive'. The struggle that inevitably ensues provides a stimulus to biological adaptations in human beings by which certain 'favourable modifications' are preserved and other 'injurious variations' are eliminated. In *The Descent of Man*, published twelve years later, Darwin followed the logic of Malthus when he asserted that human beings shared certain traits with other animals lower down the evolutionary scale. His boundless sexual appetites made 'man' a predatory and bestial creature, one controlled by his own nature (Young 1969: 109–41; Bowler 1976: 631–50).

Advocacy of Malthus' doctrine of 'moral restraint' became an acceptable expression of early Victorian anxiety about sexuality and reproduction. A feminist of sorts, John Stuart Mill blamed men's vile 'animal functions' for the subjugation of women. Sentencing women to sexual servitude for life, the marriage contract permitted husbands to assert their 'conjugal rights' over wives. Within his own private life, Mill aspired to become a civilized 'man of reason' by repressing uncontrollable bodily desires and biological functions. He described his own childless marriage as an ideal domestic arrangement, a transcendent sexless partnership between equal persons who shared intellectual interests. In chapter after chapter of his *Principles of Political Economy*, published in 1845, Mill revealed his middle-class prejudices against the overly prolific poor. He preached about how tragic it was that the lower orders produced such a 'devastating torrent of babies' (Rose 1984: 95–140).

Despite the belief that 'man' was a victim of animal instincts, people did have some power over reproduction. Birth control was an established custom among the European nobility well before the onset of industrialization. Landed families who wished to secure wealth for future generations rigidly controlled family size through celibacy, marriage postponement, primogeniture and contractual unions. And peasants too regularly practised family planning in order to protect patrimony from the division of land among too many heirs. In rural households, herbal medicines, postpartum taboos and extended nursing allowed women to space births and thereby decrease their reproductive output (McLaren 1978: ch. 1). Late marriage and early death also acted as checks on population growth. Despite the prevalence of traditional forms of birth control, high fertility and high mortality still prevailed in early modern rural societies. But in the course of the nineteenth century, a momentous 'demographic revolution' began as the old sexual regime gave way to a new pattern of fertility and mortality.

During the years from about 1850 to 1950, a new population system emerged as developing societies underwent a shift towards ever decreasing fertility and mortality. Historians still disagree about the causes of this important social change. Some believe that a 'revolution' in sentiments about love and intimacy within marriage occurred during this period. Edward Shorter, for example, attributes the pronounced decrease in marital fertility in the nineteenth century to the alleged rise of more 'modern' attitudes about sex. A diffusion of contraceptive knowledge and techniques among the working classes, he believes, gave women more control over their bodies and sexually emancipated them (Shorter 1971: 261–9 and 1976). Others contend that expectations of higher living standards may have given an impetus to family planning among the new middle classes, but that largely economic factors lay behind the practice of birth control among the proletariat (Tilly *et al.* 1976: 447–77; Fairchilds 1978: 627–69). Waged workers did benefit from better, more affordable housing, public sanitation, medical services and food supplies which all contributed towards an improvement in life expectancy. The rise of the new factory system undermined the traditional household economy of the *ancien régime* which was dependent on the maintenance of high fertility. As nations industrialized, children were no longer perceived as a valuable source of labour for the family (Tilly and Scott 1978). Lower infant and adult mortality, coupled with decreased rates of child labour due to the expansion of secondary education and the enactment of protective factory legislation, gave an impetus to couples to limit the number of their offspring.

In France, this transition to a life-cycle pattern more common to modern societies began earlier and lasted longer than it did in any other European nation. This has led historians like Angus McLaren to question the relevance of economic arguments about the causes of fertility decline (McLaren 1983: ch. 1). Since France underwent a relatively belated and slow process of industrialization, he points out, 'modernization' cannot be considered as the only factor behind the demographic transition. In answer to McLaren's objections, avoidance of any monocausal explanation for fertility decline seems most sensible. A combination of social and economic forces undoubtedly accounted for the shift.

By the end of the nineteenth century, new, more reliable statistics showed that many countries shared the experience of a decline in births and deaths. Some people must have chosen to control births because of higher expectations of affluence. Others were probably motivated primarily by economic factors. Whatever the reasons, married fertility did fall dramatically as the new social classes created by industrial capitalism practised family planning on a large scale. Not only did the bourgeoisie consciously limit the number of their children, but also the proletariat had recourse to abortion and contraception. Changes in the technology, production and distribution of contraceptives occurred during this period as new diaphragms, condoms, sponges and pessaries hit a growing middle-class market. Birth control information and devices also became more readily available to the educated and wealthy. Doctors discreetly published manuals outlining contraceptive techniques under such titles as *Married Love* and *Family Hygiene*. Chemists freely sold substances like quinine, which could be used as a spermicide or as an abortifacient, and magazines carried advertisements for agencies offering services for 'female menstrual complaints', a commonplace veiled reference to abortionists and their remedies. But many of the available, so-called 'artificial' methods of birth control were too prohibitively expensive for the working class.

For working-class women, illegal abortion became an increasingly common form of birth control. Most women attempted to abort by inserting instruments, for example, hairpins, into their wombs. Others procured cheap but dangerous abortions through wise women and midwives. Those who chose an abortion often faced illness, injury or death as a consequence of accident, incompletion and infection. Traditional methods of birth control also persisted in an industrial age since knowledge about which drugs were likely to induce miscarriage was passed down from one generation to the next. Women attempted to bring on menstruation by means of a full range of strenuous activities, as well as abortifacients, including herbal potions and post-coital douches. Couples wishing to prevent unwanted pregnancy could also abstain from sex and have intercourse only at safe periods. And probably the most prevalent, if not the most effective, form of birth control, the withdrawal method, had the advantage of being free (Knight 1977: 57–82).

Some sexual reformers welcomed the emergence of new reproductive attitudes and 'modern' patterns of childbearing. The rediscovery of Malthus led to the rise of so-called 'neo-Malthusianism', a world-wide movement which advocated prudent planning as a way to restrict population growth to levels which did not outstrip the subsistence capability of families or nations. 'Neo-Malthusians' argued that even in an industrial age, which had engendered a seemingly unlimited expansion in economic resources, national income, and the global trade in foodstuffs, a sudden or continuous rise in population would lead to declining living standards and a lower quality of life. Unrestrained population increase, they believed, adversely affected family budgets, labour markets and national economies and resulted in a subsistence crisis which even affluent and industrialized countries could not comfortably sustain. As a result of these and other beliefs, birth control movements arose in many different nations, beginning in the 1860s when a society was initially founded in England. Although their first league floundered from a lack of funds, as well as from an initially tiny and ever dwindling membership, the small group which comprised the English 'neo-Malthusian' movement formed another one in 1877. The new league immediately began a very public campaign to spread information about contraception and, by the 1880s, it had succeeded in gaining the public support of some physicians, politicians and even clergymen (D'Arcy 1977: 429–48).

Societies also sprang up elsewhere on the Continent as sexual reformers began to organize and agitate on behalf of the cause of enlightened parenthood: in 1889 in Germany; 1896 in France; 1904 in Spain; 1906 in Belgium; 1908 in Switzerland; 1911 in Sweden, and 1913 in Italy. From 1900 to 1927, birth controllers increased contacts with activists in other countries and participated in seven international conferences culminating in a huge gathering in Geneva (Noonan 1966: 406–7). Although 'neo-Malthusians' never openly endorsed the practice of such controversial methods of birth control as abortion, they still faced public hostility and political repression. That parenthood should be 'planned' seemed a contravention of 'natural' and 'divine' law to many. Moreover, Malthus' now somewhat outmoded notion of 'moral restraint' did not transgress conventional morality; indeed the idea was predicated on religious belief. But advocacy of birth control by means of 'artificial' devices elicited such vehement opposition because it seemed to license promiscuity and immorality. Support for movements also tended to come from an assortment of radicals – anarchists, syndicalists, socialists, feminists and libertarians – all committed idealists who loudly proclaimed birth control to be an instrument of sexual liberation for women and men and socio-economic liberation for the working class. As a result, many middle-class conservatives determined to combat what they perceived to be a revolutionary threat by launching their own fierce crusades to protect the public from the depravity of fanatics. They rallied in increasing numbers to uphold the sexual status quo and Victorian social values by forming societies devoted to defending 'the family', 'motherhood' and 'morality'.

Competing visions of the social and sexual order struggled for public acceptance. Birth controllers risked censure and imprisonment by publishing material about contraception which aimed at spreading the message that people should limit the size of their families for the sake of themselves, their families and their nation. In retaliation, self-styled 'anti-Malthusians' widely publicized their own views that national wealth, personal happiness and family welfare could increase only if population grew substantially. By the end of the nineteenth century, a battle over births began as the issue of fertility control provoked intense debate within the Church, the academic world, civil society and the political establishment. Contemporaries did not fail to notice that the practice of birth control separated sexuality from reproduction and gave women control over their bodies and lives. Progressives welcomed women's freedom from the tyranny of unavoidable pregancy, while conservatives feared that increasing numbers of newly emancipated females would destroy the two pillars of the social order, the institutions of marriage and motherhood. Those who stood on opposite sides of the demographic battlefield either acclaimed or decried the alleged 'epidemic' of abortion and the 'birth strike' perpetrated by 'modern' women who refused to bear many babies for their nation.

A number of factors conspired to give the upper hand to the 'anti-Malthusian' pronatalist cause. Birth controllers could find few recruits among a public painfully aware of the fact that Malthus' dire prediction of impending 'over-population' had not come true. In fact, the continuous decrease in fertility in the last decades of the nineteenth century caused another major shift in attitudes about population. Although experienced to varying degrees by different countries, the precipitous fall in the birthrate after 1870 eclipsed fears about over-breeding and provoked panic about 'depopulation'. The most visible outcome of this change in outlook was the proliferation in many different nations of a vast range of alarmist literature on the immanent threat of demographic extinction. A general anxiety about 'degeneration' emerged at the end of the nineteenth century as many industrialized nations faced the grim reality of a shrinking birthrate.

Malthus' fear of over-population no longer seemed relevant to observers who worried about dwindling national strength and efficiency. The menace of 'depopulation' also became a subject of medical and scientific study as experts from many different disciplines explored its causes and consequences. Academic debate about fertility decline became intertwined with wider concerns about the future of the family, the nation and the economy which the educated public and politicians from different parties shared. A haunting sense of decadence and decay pervaded late nineteenth-century culture and politics. Alarmists used terms like 'sterility' and 'impotence' to invoke deep-seated fears about the disastrous consequences of 'infecundity' for great powers in an age of industry and empire. For political leaders as much as for distinguished intellectuals, the drop in the birthrate threatened to endanger the nation's prospects for continued prosperity and progress.

In each nation covered in this study, the 'population question' reflected native preoccupations. The terms and causes of the debate over fertility also differed in each country. The widespread alarm over a diminishing birthrate reveals much about changing perceptions of national grandeur and decline. Common to many different societies, panic over 'depopulation' discloses much about the nature and varieties of nationalism at the dawn of a new millennium. Demographic debate in Italy arose in the context of a crisis of the liberal state. In the aftermath of unification, many nationalists became painfully aware of the frailties of Italian nationhood. A newly arising nation, Italy was the least imperial of all of Europe's great powers. Unable to solve Italy's own economic and political problems, the kingdom's ruling class made the conquest of empire a top priority for government. An aggressive campaign that lasted eleven years began in 1885 when an Italian expedition first landed at Massawa, the principal port of Eritrea. A protracted colonial war culminated in the defeat of the Italian army at Adowa in 1896, an embarrassing incident which crushed aspirations to acquire all of Ethiopia. The humiliation provoked an outcry among frustrated nationalists who saw it as a symptom of the newly unified kingdom's precocious 'degeneration'. In Italy, the beginnings of the fertility debate coincided with a resurgence of nationalism and colonialism at the end of the century. The 'population question' fed into the politics of vindication which resulted in renewed attempts at expansionism in East Africa. Pronatalists stirred longstanding ambitions for a New Roman Empire which finally found an outlet in 1911 when the Italian army invaded Libya. France underwent cultural crisis and political upheaval after the Franco-Prussian War of 1870–1 ended in victory for an expansionist Germany. The rise of a powerful new German empire awakened increased anxiety about the Third Republic's fitness for the future. France seemed to many to be on the point of extinction. Bismarck created colonies in West Africa and the Pacific in the years 1884–5, but plans for more *Lebensraum* seemed doomed by a dwindling birthrate.

The rise of a New World Order intensified international rivalry and militant nationalism. Nationalists associated wealth with the possession of empire. Their cries that the 'mother country' had to be populous in order to create colonies and protect dominion caused many to forsake their beliefs in 'neo-Malthusianism' by the end of the nineteenth century. Japan underwent a process of accelerated industrialization and imperial expansion after 1868 which transformed it into an economic giant and a major power. Japanese aspirations in Southeast Asia resulted in deteriorating relations with China, ending ultimately in the outbreak of a Sino-Japanese war in 1894. News of Japan's modernized army and its resounding victory in 1895 destroyed any remaining complacency about lasting European supremacy in global affairs. Statesmen began to contemplate the possibility that a 'White Europe' weakened by 'depopulation' could easily be conquered by the prolific 'Yellow Races' of the Far East. Britain's repeated attempts to extend its control of South Africa beyond the Cape led to two Anglo-Boer wars in 1881–2 and 1899–1902 which demonstrated just how bloody the fight for empire could be. The eventual defeat of the Boers in 1902 did not abate fears about the nation's imperial destiny. After the cessation of hostilities, an Interdepartmental Committee on Physical Deterioration carried out an official inquiry which revealed that a large number of the men who had volunteered to fight in 1899–1902 had been refused entry into the army because of their low height and poor health. These results gave grave cause for worry about the nation's fitness for the future. Theodore Roosevelt hardly welcomed the influx of Asian, Italian and Jewish immigrants into the United States which began in the 1880s. In 1905, he warned of the 'race suicide' of America's ruling class of Anglo-Saxon Protestants. The growing 'differential birthrate' between blacks and whites and the 'Yellow Peril' coming from the Orient threatened to undermine the basis of US power, he believed. The President urged 'native' Americans (meaning white and middle class) to replenish themselves by having more babies.

Analysis of the causes and consequences of birthrate decline also provoked discussion of a whole range of issues relating to 'the social question' and public health. The quality, as well as the quantity, of population became the focus of much concern. The fertility debate had an impact in the development of established sciences, like economics and anthropology, and in the advancement of new areas of research, such as the study of nutrition and sexuality. The threat of impending 'demographic degeneration' also inspired experts from many different branches of science and medicine to propose strategies aimed at 'regenerating' society. Men of science and medicine saw themselves as the guardians of the future with a mission to apply their knowledge socially for the common good. They diagnosed social ills such as criminality, alcoholism and prostitution, and prescribed biological remedies to halt the transmission of these 'defects' to succeeding generations. Some argued in favour of limiting the fertility of undesirable elements within the working class who allegedly endangered the nation's health by having too many offspring of an 'inferior' type. Others advocated that the state should promote birthrate increase by means of procreative incentives and welfare reforms. A variety of plans for prospective population policies emerged out of initial anxiety over the birthrate.

Eugenicists stood at the forefront of these debates about demographic degeneration. The history of eugenics began in 1883 when the English mathematician, Francis Galton, coined the word from a Greek root meaning 'noble in heredity'. A cousin of Charles Darwin, Galton described eugenics as a new science whose social application would lead to the betterment of humanity. Eugenics, he explained, was the study of 'the agencies under social control that may improve or impair racial qualities' (Kevles 1985: ix). He maintained that society should not leave evolution to chance but that scientists should help governments to implement policies aimed at engineering biological improvements in people. The time had come, he believed, to interfere in the slow process of 'natural selection' which Charles Darwin had discovered. Influenced by Darwin, Galton was none the less aware of the fact that the theory of natural selection did not fully explain the mechanisms for the transmission of individual traits from parents to their offspring. In his first edition of *The Origin of Species* in 1859, Darwin wrote that the 'laws of inheritance are quite unknown' (Bennett 1983: 2; Haller 1963: 4, 8 and 17). Darwin had guessed that environmental conditions could provoke adaptations in organisms which were inheritable, but he never provided an adequate explanation of how this was so. Galton's main concern, therefore, was to advance understanding of evolution and heredity with a view to producing 'favourable' variations and thereby improving human stock. He and his followers spoke confidently, far too prematurely so, about the ability of scientists to tamper with evolution and to conquer nature itself through what they called 'artificial selection', a term meaning the conscious cultivation of 'desirable' human attributes and the extermination of 'unsuitable' ones. Eugenicists believed that it would be possible in the near future to create a 'highly gifted race' by selecting the best inborn qualities of individuals and encouraging them to prevail by means of 'sound breeding'. They proposed that the 'hereditarily unworthy' should be prevented from propagating and that the 'biologically superior' should be persuaded to give birth to more children.

Eugenics, then, emerged as an outgrowth of interest in evolution and heredity. It grew out of a new veneration for science which became increasingly visible in culture and politics from the 1860s. Many came to believe that the crowning achievement of the nineteenth century was the conquest of 'superstition', embodied in adherence to religious doctrine, which advances in scientific knowledge had caused. Faith in science became the new secular creed for an age which worshipped progress, reason and evolution as the instruments of Utopia. Eugenics was also one facet of a much broader phenomenon, the rise of what historians have called 'Social Darwinism', a new system of thought and representation which emerged as a consequence of the ascendancy of evolutionism. Much has been written about Social Darwinism and not all of it has been helpful. Social Darwinism can best be seen as a new way of looking at the world which took as its guiding principle that human society was analogous to that of even the most primitive biological organisms. The Darwinist theory of evolution and selection stood at the centre of Social Darwinism, a movement in the history of ideas whose adherents claimed that society was an organism which was subject to the natural laws that Darwin had discovered. The language of the 'struggle for existence' did dominate many Social Darwinist writings about the inevitability of militarism, imperialism and capitalism. The social order was seen as one in which competition, rivalry and war were 'natural'. The 'selectionist' arguments of Social Darwinists could also be used as grounds for opposition to welfare reform. According to some strands of 'Social Darwinism', welfare programmes were harmful to the race because they benefited the least 'fit' among the population and they interfered in the processes of natural selection. By supplying seemingly incontrovertible 'scientific' proof for the existence of a 'natural' hierarchy among races, Social Darwinism also had serious political implications in the development of modern racist and supremacist belief. But Social Darwinism, like eugenics, was not simply an elaborate scientific rationale for a platform of right-wing ideas. Many scholars have recognized that Social Darwinists could be liberals, feminists and socialists, as well as reactionaries, racists and fascists (Halliday 1971: 389–406).

This faith in science as the guardian of the future, most scholars would agree, lay at the heart of eugenics. A new generation of thinkers flirted with the idea that an individual's behaviour and characteristics could indeed be modified according to precise scientific specifications. Because of the inflated claims made for it by enthusiasts, the movement quickly gained followers throughout the industrialized and developing world. In the first decades of the twentieth century, societies were founded in scores of countries as far afield as the United States, Japan, South Africa, France, Germany, Brazil, Italy, the Soviet Union, Hungary, Mexico and Turkey (Nisot 1929: vol. II, introduction). Founded in 1907, the English Eugenics Education Society presided over the first international eugenics conference at London University in July 1912. Hundreds of delegates from different nations attended the meeting. The Rt. Hon. Winston Churchill, the First Lord of the Admiralty, and Charles William Elliot, a former president of Harvard University, were both vice-presidents of the congress. Alfred Ploetz, president of the German Race Hygiene Society, and Sir William Osler, Regius Professor of Medicine at Oxford University, joined a long list of distinguished guests (*Problems in Eugenics* 1912: vol. I, xi).

During his address at the inaugural dinner, the Rt. Hon. A.J. Balfour gave a spirited defence of eugenics by calling it 'the first great applied science'. But he also urged its followers to be modest in their aims. Too much was still unknown about heredity, he warned, for eugenicists to sustain the illusion that they could perfect human beings and 'bring the millennium upon earth'. Eugenicists should also beware of extremists within their ranks who wished to impose their own vision of what constituted an ideal society. Because of its apparent applicability, eugenics could easily lead to the abuse of scientific knowledge by those with immoral ends. Eugenicists were partly to blame for the appropriation of their ideas by 'faddists' since they made inflated claims 'dangerously, incautiously, and casually'. Darwin had used the word 'fit', he elaborated, only to describe an organism's adaptability to its surroundings. But in scientific and popular usage the word had now come to be invested with all sorts of 'unscientific' meanings. Eugenicists, he explained, should never employ 'fitness' to mean those traits which they themselves perceived to be 'desirable'. Scientists, he clarified, should never attribute to nature any intentions. Nor should they make subjective judgements about which human characteristics were worthy of preservation and which were most definitely not. To do so would be unethical (*Problems in Eugenics* 1913: vol. II, 7–9).

Balfour was unusually sensitive to the implications of eugenics. He struggled with the realization that eugenics threatened an individual's rights to reproduce without interference from science and the state. Far more common was the uncritical approbation which Leonard Darwin heaped on delegates. In his address, Leonard Darwin, the second youngest of Charles Darwin's five sons and Galton's successor as president of the English Eugenics Education Society, welcomed the 'universal acceptance of the principle of evolution in all fields of knowledge'. Eugenics was but the 'practical application of the evolutionary principle'. His father, he stated, had proven beyond any reasonable doubt that biology was destiny. Although the laws of inheritance remained a mystery, Darwin admitted, the task facing eugenicists was to convince the public and politicians alike that urgent reforms were needed to protect posterity. A new politics must be created, one which worked in partnership with science and recognized that issues such as the welfare of the unborn child were of paramount importance to the nation and the state. The biggest question facing the twentieth century, he added, was whether society would have the courage to safeguard the human race and promote 'moral and physical progress' by implementing policies for 'conscious selection' (*Problems in Eugenics* 1984: 1–6).

At the 1912 conference, eugenicists discussed a number of ways to promote biological improvements to the race. Chief among these were so-called 'negative' measures for the strict regulation of fertility. These comprised plans to segregate the mentally and physically handicapped for life, to forbid unhealthy people from marrying (an idea which Galton had named 'selective marriages'), to create a female caste of 'highly select' reproducers to service the nation, to legalize polygamy for particularly superior specimens of manhood (an idea which George Bernard Shaw embraced passionately), to compel the working class to practise birth control, to sterilize the biologically 'unfit' and to murder *en masse* the racially unsound. In addition to these 'negative' eugenic remedies, proposals for so-called 'positive' eugenics to encourage births were also made. These included an extension of statutory welfare and social security provision, the introduction of a welter of laws favouring large families and the enactment of tax reforms penalizing the unmarried and childless (Quine 1990: 18–20).

These ideas would gain currency in the twentieth century as concern over the optimum 'quality' and 'quantity' of population grew. As a new generation began to flirt with the idea that science could change the course of evolution, politicians began to listen to calls to implement policies aimed at altering sexuality and fertility. The countries covered in this survey all ultimately implemented programmes based on the principle that social intervention could influence the birthrate. Radically different kinds of governments in Italy, France and Germany launched population policies inspired by both 'negative' and 'positive' eugenics. A belief in the applicability of science to society was the foundation for these programmes. And a hope that people's behaviour and characteristics could be modified according to precise scientific specifications motivated states to tamper with human development by means of 'artificial selection'.

The adoption of population policies, therefore, was an important episode in the history of the modern state at a time when it began to apply scientific ideas to social policies. When Mussolini stood before his parliament and people in 1927 to launch his pronatalist demographic campaign, he stated that he wished above all else to correct those evolutionary errors which had made Italians such a dying and degenerate race. He aimed to 'cure' society of such ills as alcoholism, pauperism and criminality, which slowed the forward advance of the race towards the predestined recreation of empire. This desire to promote national regeneration and resurrection through population planning was not confined to a fascist dictatorship. Statesmen throughout Europe and elsewhere also shared a belief that the state should intervene in the private sphere in order to promote desirable biological and social change. An authoritarian 'biological politics' was born out of a partnership between science, medicine and the state.

Mussolini and other leaders of the new activist governments which arose in the twentieth century sought mastery over the upward march of humankind. The modern state, in both its democratic and fascist forms, employed eminently authoritarian policies to extend rule over the domain of domestic life by regulating the family, sexuality, reproduction and parenting. Personal choices and freedoms became political issues of critical importance to politicians seeking to safeguard the national interest by altering fertility. This book aims to give an account of the origins and impact of the profound shift in attitudes which accompanied birthrate decline in different nations. The growth of social, medical, women's and gender histories has increased interest in this important topic. Research into the relationship between state and society and the links between public and private spheres has emerged in recent years. But with few exceptions, many of the new studies on this subject are locked into national perspectives. This book seeks to provide a synthesis of recent work and to place the problem in a comparative focus. It traces the early history of those infringements on our power over our own bodies which have become such an enduring feature of twentieth-century biological politics of all persuasions.

1   From Malthus to Mussolini

Fascist Italy's 'battle for births'

> No one today can take the notorious, would-be 'law' of Malthus
> at all seriously. . . . It is absurd to think that a decreasing birthrate
> will improve the living standards of the Italian people.
>
> (Benito Mussolini. From his essay entitled 'Numbers as force',
> which first appeared in print in 1928)

Italian fertility during the years 1870–1945 gave no cause for com-
plaint. In many countries, an eighteenth-century average of around
forty live births per 1,000 of the total population started to descend
in the late nineteenth century and finally reached about twenty by
the early twentieth century. Britain, and Germany to a lesser extent,
fit this pattern of ever rapid decline in the decades after 1870. Italy,
however, did not share this experience. The drop in the kingdom's
birthrate began after 1890 and was hardly precipitous thereafter.
Italian natality still stood at 36.8 in the period 1870–2, remained
well above thirty throughout the prewar period, and only slowly
dwindled to 23.1 in the years 1930–2. Not until after 1945 did levels
fall below twenty. And, somewhat exceptionally, at no time during
this demographic shift did the Italian birthrate ever sink below the
deathrate (Bacci 1980: 80; Bacci and Breschi 1990: 385–408).

The peculiar distinction of Italy during this downturn was the
kingdom's still healthy prospect for continued demographic expansion. After 1914, governments world-wide grew increasingly worried
about the birthrate because of the unprecedented toll of casualties
caused by the First World War. An estimated 765,400 British soldiers
lost their lives during the hostilities. After three years of combat,
680,070 Italian servicemen were reported either killed or missing in
action. And as many as 1,393,515 men died while defending France.
Rising rates of sickness among the civilian population also prompted

public debate. The sheer magnitude of death and destruction caused by total war provoked concern about the 'population question'.

In the postwar period, the numerical preponderance of women over men, and of old people over young people, drove the birth, fertility and marriage rates far below prewar levels. In Britain, statesmen understood only too well that the birthrate fell by 50 per cent between 1900 and 1930, and that over three-quarters of this diminution occurred after 1914. French observers were also painfully aware of the huge 'deficit' in births. Without heavy immigration during the years 1921 to 1930, the French population would not have grown nearly as much as it did. Many belligerent nations did not experience any pronounced fertility upswings after the cessation of war. But Italy saw its birthrate bounce back vigorously after 1918 when natality reached an all-time low of eighteen. By 1920, the Italian birthrate rose to 31.8 as a result of a boom in marriages and babies (Glass and Blacker 1939: 11–26). Although this brief upturn did not arrest the long-term momentum of demographic decline, it was an index of the country's continued commitment to the perpetuation of the population.

Italians were in fact propagating at an exceptional rate despite the postwar odds. In marked contrast, the French had long since renounced a lively birthrate as a cause of population increase. The French birthrate started to plummet around 1740, when other nations like Italy, Britain and Germany were experiencing the first signs of a prolonged boom in births. In France, natality was already as low as 30.8 in 1821–30 and 27.4 in 1841–50. The rate plunged further to 26.2 in 1876, 18.8 in 1911–13 and 9.5 in 1916 (McLaren 1983: 25 and 169; Ogden and Huss 1982: 285). Moreover, during this period of decline, deaths exceeded births in a number of years. France had more reason than any other European nation to worry about becoming a moribund people. Far from facing any threat of imminent depopulation, however, Italy actually seemed to be suffering from a veritable 'Malthusian' crisis of over-population. Acute demographic pressure on limited economic resources condemned the bulk of the Italian populace to very low subsistence.

The human cost of high fertility in such an impoverished nation was high mortality. An index of low living standards, levels of infant and child mortality were much higher in Italy than they were in more wealthy nations (Hogan and Kertzer 1986: 361–85). About one-quarter of all newborn infants died during their first year of life in 1881. In 1901, only sixty-nine out of one hundred children could expect to live for ten years. In 1911, 15 per cent of babies perished before they reached the age of one and another 10 per cent failed to survive into adulthood. And prenatal and neonatal mortality actually rose after 1871. Indices of poor standards of health, nutrition and housing, these rates may have increased partly because of better medical registration. But significantly, they still did not begin to show a persistent decline until after 1945 (Del Panta 1979: 204). Another indication of population excess, about 25,000 unwanted infants were abandoned each year at convents, roadsides and churches. The deathrate of foundlings was more than double that of infants raised within families (Quine 1990: ch. 7).[1]

Italian demography reflected peculiarities in the kingdom's economic development. If industrialization is taken to mean the transference of resources from agriculture into industry, then the Italian economy was relatively backward until a later date. With most of its labour force still on the land throughout the prewar period, Italy remained an overwhelmingly rural and underdeveloped nation. As late as 1937, the proportion of the economically active population engaged in agriculture was as high as 48.1 per cent, while only 33.1 per cent worked in industry. Italy had a 'big spurt' in industrial production during the years 1896–1908, when the annual rate of growth reached 6.7 per cent (Federico and Toniolo 1992: 206–7). But the process of industrialization was slow, uneven and interrupted. Throughout the years 1870–1945, many of those who were listed in censuses as industrial workers would have toiled in small workshops employing no more than a few labourers.

After unification, the kingdom suffered from a chronic 'agrarian problem' characterized by the persistence of outmoded forms of underproductive and labour-intensive agriculture. In southern Italy, labourers worked on huge estates, called *latifundia*, which were owned by quasi-seignorial, absentee landlords. Drawn from the local nobility, proprietors owned not only the means of production but also most of the crop. Productivity was low given the extensive cultivation of land, the poor quality of the soil, the intemperate climate, the lack of investment and the primitive nature of farming technique. The *latifundo* economy proved to be thoroughly unable to keep food production in pace with prodigious population pressure (Serpieri 1930: 12–18). Because of competition for work, labour was cheap and exploited. Southern agricultural workers lived well below

---

[1] Much of this chapter is based on the research presented in my 1990 doctoral thesis, 'From Malthus to Mussolini: The Italian Eugenics Movement and Fascist Population Policy, 1890–1938'. When citations do not appear in the text of the book, the sources of the material provided can be found in the dissertation.

subsistence, and their lives were characterized by seasonal poverty, unemployment, hunger and disease. Despite the wretchedness of their condition, Southern peasants continued to have large families. Cultural rather then economic factors accounted for the maintenance of high fertility in the *Mezzogiorno*.

Because of the failure of unification to integrate the South into a new national community, the *Mezzogiorno* remained largely untouched by the processes of change affecting more advanced regions (Barbagli 1984). In the North, the modernizing influences of secularization, a shift towards industrial work, the expansion of compulsory primary education, rising literacy rates, the beginnings of labour legislation and the spread of socialism undermined traditional family structures and social relations (Musso 1988: 61–106). But in the South, the customarily large patriarchal peasant family survived well into the twentieth century (Manoukian 1988: 3–61).

Other forms of agricultural organization provided an economic rationale for high fertility. In central Italy, the dominant form of land tenure was still the archaic *mezzadria*, a system of share-cropping in which extended families lived together in multi-unit households. Under the terms of the *mezzadria* contract, the proprietor provided land and the *mezzadro* (the tenant farmer) provided labour. The landlord took a share of the crop and the remainder went to the peasant (Serpieri 1920: 84 and 89). Although it reduced labourers' living standards to a bare subsistence, share-cropping provided no incentive to limit children since it was built around the household as a unit of production. The family economy depended on the exploitation of female and child labour and the existence of a large domestic work force (Kertzer 1984; Kertzer and Hogan 1989).

Older productive and social systems survived into an industrial age. Co-existing with the *latifundia* and the *mezzadria*, highly commercialized agriculture and agro-industry did develop throughout the Po Valley (Cardoza 1979: 172–212 and 1982; Bull and Corner 1993: ch. 1). These gave rise to a class of landless day labourers. Like wage-workers in factories, *braccianti* had begun to limit fertility by the end of the nineteenth century. But because of the uneven pattern of Italian industrialization, the size of the rural and urban proletariat remained small compared to other countries. About 20 per cent of the population was classified as working class as late as the interwar period, and many of these workers were concentrated in isolated areas. The Italian peninsula and islands had few pockets of capitalist industry and agriculture which could generate new social values and reproductive habits. Located in the north-west, Piedmont, Lombardy and Liguria became known as Italy's 'industrial triangle', an oasis of large-scale production and urban development within a predominantly rural society. In Italy, regional variations in economic progress were particularly pronounced, and these differences had significant demographic consequences.

Italian demography reflected the widening economic gap between North and South after 1881. Population trends varied enormously between the more industrialized and prosperous regions of the North and Centre and the more backward and impoverished *Mezzogiorno*. A distinct pattern of 'demographic dualism' gradually arose in which the South as a whole clung to an old regime of high fertility and high mortality. The sharpest decline in births occurred in the big cities of the North where the average age at marriage was 22–4 years for women and 26–7 years for men. The drop in Italian fertility after 1890 was due mainly to the increasing tendency of younger women to concentrate births in the early years of marriage. The entrepreneurial, mercantile and professional middle classes took the lead by limiting child output in this way. The Italian working class was also beginning to redefine maternity by having fewer children and confining childbearing to briefer periods. But Italy still had no shortage of large families.

For more advanced nations like Britain, the war completed the transformation of the large Victorian family into its diminutive twentieth-century successor. Only belatedly, however, did Italy experience this demographic transition. A far better index of procreative performance than the crude birthrate, fertility quotients measure the reproductive output of the female population. By the end of the 1920s, Britain reluctantly claimed the lowest level of fertility of any Western European nation, with 56.43 births annually for every 1,000 women of childbearing age (Wrigley 1961: 144–7; Brookes 1986: 149–75). French contemporaries witnessed a no less shocking reality when their fertility ratio dropped to 67.37 by 1930 (Wrigley 1969: 158–9; 174–5; 183–7). But in 1931, the Italian kingdom still boasted an unusually high fertility rate of 95.35 births for every 1,000 women between the ages of 15 and 55 (Glass and Blacker 1939: 9).

The progressive shift towards the two-child families more typical of north-western Europe occurred only slowly in Italy. In 1928, an official census revealed that over 14 per cent of all Italian families were 'large', defined as containing at least seven children. The 1928 census also investigated class differentials in female fertility and family size. According to the results, an Italian middle-class couple had three children on average. Urban and rural wage-earners were far more prolific. Women listed in the census as wives of factory workers had produced 5.9 live children on average. And an average family of agricultural labourers comprised 6.5 children.

Nor had all Italian women even begun to confine childbearing to the early stages of their reproductive cycles. The practice of birth control was far more widespread in the nation's northern regions, and women from the South routinely produced children well into middle age. From 1880–90, millions fled the South for unskilled jobs in northern industries and foreign countries. Despite mass emigration and the preponderance of females in the population, the birthrate remained very high in the South. In Calabria, Apulia and Sicily, for example, most women married before their eighteenth birthday. And although they limited output by spacing births, many still fell pregnant at regular two or two-and-a-half-yearly intervals until they reached menopause. Not all newborn infants survived adolescence because the South was a region blighted by high unemployment, low wages and social misery. In 1928, Southerners figured prominently among the 1.5 million families with between seven and ten children and the 500,000 with ten or more. But because standards of health and welfare in the *Mezzogiorno* were among the worse in all of Europe, the premature deaths of infants and children from preventable causes remained disturbingly common. Population attrition, rather than prudent planning, somewhat limited the size of Southern families.

Recognition of the pronounced disequilibrium between population and subsistence grew. Compelling evidence of the poor living standards and quality of life of the masses renewed interest in the writings of Malthus. At the turn of the century, some liberal economists came to espouse the view that Italy had to curb population growth in order to prosper. A few members of the medical profession also began to champion the cause of 'voluntary motherhood'. Vaguely eugenic aims motivated doctors to support birth control on the grounds that too many pregnancies caused a woman to produce inferior offspring. From the 1880s on, Italian doctors showed an increased willingness to study sex and reproduction, two areas which had traditionally been the province of religion and morality. Left-wing gynaecologists published a number of 'neo-Malthusian' works describing birth control methods (De Longis 1982: 157–62), but inevitably, these reached only a tiny proportion of the 38 per cent of the population which was literate.

In 1909, a circle of progressive thinkers based in Milan decided to provoke a public debate about fertility. They sent out question-naires to prominent figures investigating attitudes towards birth control. Interestingly however, the majority of respondents vehemently rejected the principles of Malthusianism. They criticized the idea that an excess of 'prolificity' condemned the proletariat to poverty and misery. Some doctors argued that any form of birth control, including abstinence and coitus interruptus, degraded the sexual act, endangered health and violated the 'law of nature'. Among the few women who voiced an opinion, Ester Bonomi opposed contraception because she believed it would increase women's sexual servitude and economic insecurity. If Italy became a more permissive society, she contended, men would have no compulsion to marry. Moral standards would degenerate and the family would perish. Moreover, economists provided detailed arguments about why Italy should strive to increase the size of its population (Lanaro 1979: 56–7).

The unpopularity of the notion that fertility should be limited did not deter birth controllers from seeking a forum for debate. In 1910, the only prewar conference on the 'sexual question' took place in Florence. Advocates of birth control represented only a small minority of the participants. The revolutionary syndicalist, Luigi Berta, urged those present to educate the masses about contraceptive methods. He put forth a motion calling for the immediate dissemination of Malthusian propaganda among the people (Wanrooij 1990: 74). But delegates at the convention did not subject this resolution to a vote. Even committed supporters of Malthusianism were timid in their approach. They believed that any radical initiative in such a confessional nation would provoke strong opposition from the Church and its followers.

The cautiousness of neo-Malthusians is somewhat surprising, given the fact that Italian criminal law had no specific statute against the publication of information about birth control. Italian firms could also freely manufacture contraceptives, though most of these were in the form of condoms. Too prohibitively expensive for the working class, condoms were produced mainly for the armed forces and they were advertised as prophylactics against venereal disease. Chemists even sold a number of products which could be used as abortifacients in home remedies. Women could buy enema kits with or without special vaginal tubes. They gave themselves soapy hot water enemas in order to abort. And douching with readily available caustic substances was a common, though sometimes fatal, method to induce abortion. Unified Italy's first penal code, the Zanardelli Code of 1889, was moderately liberal in that it abolished capital punishment and reduced the severity of punishments for many crimes. The code made provision for abortion but not for birth control. Various clauses defined abortion as a 'crime against the person', much like infanticide and homicide, though less grave. Medical and legal strictures made a distinction between a foetus, which was defined in terms of its inability to thrive outside the womb, and an infant, seen as a fully-formed human being who enjoyed the rights of personhood. The code, accordingly, prescribed harsh sentences for abortion, including prison terms of up to four years for anyone procuring it and up to seven years for anyone performing it. But, if done without the woman's consent, the crime was punishable by a prison term of up to twelve years. Article 369 of the code, by contrast, prescribed even heavier sentences of up to twelve years for anyone found guilty of infanticide. The medical and legal professions suspected that abortion was endemic, in spite of the severity of prescribed sentences. Doctors also recognized that many apparent miscarriages which came to their attention were probably self-induced 'white abortions' in disguise. And they knew that women performed and sought late terminations, a fact which obscured somewhat the fine distinction between abortion and infanticide. Despite the gravity of the offence, few abortion cases ever came before the law, and when they did, courts were inclined to take extenuating circumstances into account. The leniency shown to offenders, however, did not derive from sympathy with the plight of women. It reflected the influence on Italian criminology of the followers of Cesare Lombroso, a theorist who believed in women's mental inferiority. The works of evolutionists who argued that women suffered from arrested development affecting the functioning of their faculties also bolstered this prevailing view. Since they were not intelligent enough to exercise intent, many maintained, women could not be held accountable for their crimes.

Because of the limitations of Italian criminal law, opponents of birth control were forced to invoke statutes safeguarding public decency. After three decades in which the reading public could easily find birth control information, a conservative backlash began. Twenty-seven thousand copies of *The Art of Not Having Children: Practical Neo-Malthusianism* were sold after its publication in 1911. Increasingly active as a national citizens' lobby with branches in the major cities, the League of Public Morality determined to stop the traffic in 'obscene and pornographic' literature. Although it was a lay organization with no political or religious affiliation, the league drew support from practising Catholics within the upper classes. In

1913, the society in Turin filed an action against the manual. A self-taught working man, Secondo Giorno, had written the tract, a work which caused no furore until Luigi Berta provided a preface for its second edition in 1912. When Giorno and Berta were brought to trial for obsenity, the Italian birth control movement finally had a *cause célèbre* similar to the famous Charles Bradlaugh and Annie Besant case in 1877, which inadvertently brought the cause of English neo-Malthusians to the attention of the general public (Glass 1967; 32–4). The Giorno and Berta trial also provided a great deal of free publicity, if not public sympathy, for the fledgling birth control campaign in Italy. Since their pamphlet could be found to contain no offensive language or illustrations, the verdict begrudgingly went in favour of the defendants. Despite the fact that the jury found the work 'immoral', they could not uphold the charge that it was obscene.

Completely exonerated, Berta and Giorno took advantage of their celebrity. Soon after the trial, they founded the *Lega Neo-Malthusiana* (the Neo-Malthusian League). For the next two years, Berta published a periodical which was entitled *Sexual Education: The Journal of Neo-Malthusianism and Eugenics*. The journal emphasized the revolutionary nature of birth control. Berta believed that neo-Malthusianism was a doctrine favouring the sexual liberation of women and the economic emancipation of the working class. Publishing information about available contraceptive devices, he determined to free the proletariat from the burden of large families and perpetual poverty. In 1913, *Sexual Education* asked readers whether they thought neo-Malthusianism was 'immoral'. The young socialist leader Benito Mussolini fully endorsed the principle of 'conscious parenthood'. In his reply, he stated that family planning was an act of 'wisdom, responsibility, and probity' which elevated man above the level of beasts (Wanrooij 1990: 79).

Although support for birth control was growing among individual socialists, libertarians and anarchists, Italian neo-Malthusianism never gained many adherents. Nor did the movement create alliances with the masses through trade unions and the socialist party. Unlike their British and German counterparts, Italian neo-Malthusians failed to develop strategies for propaganda and organization within working-class communities. Since they did not open birth control clinics, hold any meetings or publish popular pamphlets, the movement probably had no impact on the lives of ordinary citizens. Most Italians no doubt would not even have been aware of the existence of the society. They continued to learn about contraception and abortion from friends and family. The Italian society, in fact, did not function as a lobby group seeking members among prominent politicians and the general public. Notably absent among its exclusively male leadership were leading feminists, whose own nascent movement did not formally endorse the practice of birth control. Its journal also failed to attract much of a readership before the outbreak of war brought an abrupt end to the organized birth control movement in Italy.

The hostility which neo-Malthusianism generated in Italy reflected not the strength of the movement but rather the deep ambivalence felt about openly debating the social meaning of sexuality and repro-duction in a confessional nation. Conservatives feared that contra-ception would liberate women and that female sexual equality would threaten the institutions of marriage and motherhood. Progressives, on the other hand, hesitated to appeal for a new sexual ethics based on the enjoyment of reproductive choices and personal freedoms. Neo-Malthusians never abandoned the deeply embedded belief that propagation, motherhood and the family were the fabric of the social order. In fact, the Italian version of the neo-Malthusian ideal of 'prudent parenthood' did not differ dramatically from the procreative values of a society which was still steeped in Catholic dogma.

The Italian birth control movement was moderate. The most out-spoken supporter, Luigi Berta, was hardly representative of the majority of neo-Malthusians. Most did not believe that fertility should be decreased substantially. On the contrary, they were simply in favour of creating a more harmonious balance between economic resources and family size. They merely wished to reduce poverty by achieving an 'optimum' level of population growth. They would have been horrified at the thought that Italy should adopt the 'two-child system' prevalent in less 'fecund' nations like France and Britain. The only real difference between neo-Malthusians and pro-natalists in Italy was that advocates of birth control believed that some degree of limitation was necessary in order to relieve the general pressure of population on the means of subsistence. Only a few neo-Malthusians advocated anything so radical as the de-criminalization of abortion. And many were in favour of rather quaint but unrealistic reforms in sexual practice and social customs, such as the abolition of prostitution, premarital chastity and fidelity within marriage. Malthus would have been proud of the sexual purity campaign undertaken by some prominent Italian neo-Malthu-sians. Their appeal to middle-class men to exercise 'moral restraint' was vocal but hardly influential.

Of far more cultural and political significance, Italian pronatalism consisted entirely of a strong 'anti-Malthusian' streak which became increasingly visible in the writings of intellectuals at the turn of the century. While neo-Malthusianism never had more than a superficial impact on élite and popular culture, pronatalism became a pervasive and powerful social force in prewar Italy. Significantly too, Italian eugenics emerged as an outgrowth of pronatalism. This overlapping of eugenic and pronatalist thought in Italy had profound implications for the development of population policy during the fascist dictatorship.

Italian eugenicists rejected forms of fertility control advocated in the United States, Britain and Germany. They were opposed to 'negative' eugenic proposals for the so-called voluntary sterilization of the 'unfit' on scientific and moral grounds. Unlike their Anglo-Saxon and Nordic colleagues who favoured 'selective' breeding, Italian eugenicists wished to encourage the working class to reproduce even more prolifically. They also came to depict Italian racial superiority in terms of innate sexual prowess, libidinousness and prolificity. A distinctly Italian eugenics arose which was both Catholic and Latin in outlook.

Pronatalist and welfarist in orientation, Italian eugenics shaped the fascist demographic campaign. The imperative of population increase figured as the principal motive behind all major social and institutional initiatives launched after the consolidation of Mussolini's dictatorship in 1927. With the official proclamation that year of the beginning of a 'fecund decade', the regime determined to stimulate growth despite the enduring reality of hardship and poverty for many families. The onset first of a monetary crisis in 1927 and then a long depression in 1929 may have exposed the shortcomings of this aim, but fascism persisted none the less in its frantic bid to boost the birthrate.

The ideas which informed Mussolini's population policy predated fascism. Pronatalism emerged at the end of the century when patriotic intellectuals confronted the shortcomings of Italian nationhood after unification. After the heroic wars of independence in the years 1848–70, the new Italian kingdom seemed especially prosaic. Liberal Italy was a nation with a fragile central state, a corrupt political system and a backward economy. Deeply divided by class and regional loyalties, Italians, moreover, appeared to lack both a national and a civic consciousness. The educated élite began to see the *Risorgimento* (resurrection) as an incomplete revolution which brought mere political union but not real national unification. A new nationalism emerged out of this crisis of the liberal state.

The kingdom's second-rate status as a great power became a major concern of Italian intellectuals. While France and Britain ruled vast territories, Italy remained deprived of colonies despite repeated attempts to regain a Mediterranean empire. In 1885, the Italian government launched an expedition which resulted in the establishment of a protectorate over Eritrea four years later. This marked the beginning of eleven years of aggressive but unsuccessful Italian imperialism in East Africa. The staggering defeat of the Italian army at Adowa in 1896 by poorly-armed Ethiopian tribesmen was widely perceived as a national disaster. Frustrated imperial aspirations lay behind much of eugenic pronatalism in prewar Italy.

In a book published in 1900, Italy's most distinguished anthropologist chose the theme of national degeneration. The idea of degeneration reflected the growing belief that evolution could be regressive as well as progressive. Guiseppe Sergi (1841–1936) saw the worse symptoms of Italy's decline in the 'innate inferiority' of the nation's own governing class. Liberal leaders had propelled the country into a 'precocious decadence'. These 'political cretins', he charged, were unfit to rule what seemed destined to be an 'infantile nation' in a world dominated by superior powers. The post-unitary state was 'invalid' and 'impotent'; and political life was 'atrophied' and 'morbid'. Nowhere was the 'congenital weakness' of Italy's body politic more evident than in the crashing defeats of foreign policy. Expensive and unprofitable colonial campaigns in East Africa had exposed the 'latent paralysis' of the entire parliamentary system (Quine 1990: 21–3).

Italy had consistently blundered in the world arena and repeated humiliation had prematurely stunted the nation's imperial growth. Sergi did envisage a future, however, when a New Italy would achieve the economic and military maturity requisite for imperial conquest. In another work published in 1900, Sergi introduced race into the argument. He defined race as the biological, moral and psychic inheritance of the Italian people. Race for him constituted the most important factor for evolution. He portrayed the world as a natural order regulated by the struggle for survival between superior species and their inferior prey. Although the Italian people possessed unique moral and physical attributes, what really made them different from other less evolved races, Sergi argued, was their instinctual drive to create empire. Their Roman forebears had once brought civilization, culture and commerce to the world. Italians would once again rise to become a proud people in their predestined course of evolution. The 'Italic race' was driven by what he saw as an innate tendency towards empire (Quine 1990: 24–5).

Sergi aimed to show how militarism, imperialism and capitalism were irresistible expressions of racial temperament and destiny. The inborn qualities that he attributed to the Italian race reflected his own hopes for the future. At the turn of the century, the 'discovery' of biological race by scientists like Sergi transformed Italian nationalism by giving the struggle for empire a lofty purpose and a scientific justification in evolutionary theory. Sergi consistently depicted the Italian people as an innately warrior race whose earliest ancestors had transmitted not just unique physical characteristics but also special psychic drives. He argued that like their ancient Roman forebears present-day Italians had a 'latent' disposition which drove them to colonize and civilize lesser races. Given the political implications of his scientific works, the fascist regime later vulgarized and popularized the theories of Sergi. Borrowing directly from Sergi, Mussolini himself repeatedly described Italians as a proud and prolific people with a noble Roman pedigree. And the architects of fascist racism also openly acknowledged their debt to Sergi. Contributors to the periodical, *Razza e Civiltà* (Race and Civilization) became the official spokesmen for fascist population policy after it became explicitly racist in the late 1930s. They proclaimed Sergi as Italy's first 'great racist', an anthropologist who had proved scientifically that Italians were a superior Latin and Mediterranean race. Considered to be a 'precursor' by fascists, Sergi gave scientific credence to the regime's racism (Cenna 1940: 44).

Scholars have often underestimated the importance of racism to fascist ideology and policy before 1938. The adoption of a racial anti-Semitic policy in the summer of 1938 is also seen either as a defensive response to German claims of Nordic superiority or as a result of Nazi pressure to conform after the Rome–Berlin Axis in 1937 (Bernardini 1977: 449). But Italy had a flourishing racialist tradition long before the advent of fascism, and Sergi's influence on fascist thinking is especially evident in the wording of the regime's *Manifesto of Italian Racism* (Delzell 1971: 174–76). The actual authors of the document were prominent eugenicists who plundered Sergi's works for their definition of biological race.

In 1912, Guiseppe Sergi founded the Italian Eugenic Society along with Corrado Gini, the kingdom's most famous pronatalist. The first to popularize demography in Italy, Gini was influenced by the works of evolutionists like Charles Darwin and Herbert Spencer. He understood populations to be constantly changing and he applied this evolutionary perspective to every aspect of the human condition. As evolution progressed, he maintained, human beings became ever more physiologically advanced than lower animals, just as society and culture became increasingly differentiated. Another major source for his ideas was the belief of Malthus that a fierce struggle for survival ensued as populations grew. Like other Italian pronatalists, Gini was an 'anti-Malthusian' who criticized the notion that all organisms have a tendency to reproduce prolifically.

Published in 1912, Gini's *Demographic Factors in the Evolution of Nations* attempted to give pronatalism some scientific credibility. Demography, he maintained, was an exacting statistical discipline out of which arose understanding of the fundamental laws of population change. One of these was the premise that all populations pass through a predestined cycle of birth, growth and decay. During periods of birthrate increase, 'young' nations had a plentiful supply of workers and soldiers with which to build civilization, industry and empire. With fertility decline came the collapse of all the best that highly evolved but 'aged' societies had produced. Falling birthrates all over in Europe, but especially in France, confirmed that the fateful stage of 'demographic degeneration' had already begun (Quine 1990: 47–9).

Gini's evolutionism was quite explicitly biological. The cause of population decline, he argued, lay not in social factors like birth control and late marriage but in a decrease in the race's reproductive fitness which accompanied evolutionary progress. According to him, innate fertility deteriorated as human beings progressed beyond the primitives. This 'natural law' of population, he argued, explained why birthrates differed so much by class. The working classes were more prolific than the upper and middle classes because they were less advanced along the evolutionary scale. Gini placed no negative value judgement on the fact that the 'lower orders' were not highly evolved. On the contrary, he defined the proletariat as a 'robust' and 'virile' class which produced more offspring than the 'senile' and 'sterile' upper orders.

But since the capacity to reproduce diminished along with evolutionary advance, all Italians were losing their sex drive and instinct to propagate. They were suffering from the decreased virility characteristic of a noble but aged race. The only hope for survival that Italy had was to increase the 'fecundity' of the working class (Quine 1990: 29–30). The obvious question which arises about Gini's theory is why humanity had not perished long ago if fertility decreased with the passage of each generation. But less important than logic was the fact that Gini's premise allowed him to refute Malthus' postulate that population growth was inevitable.

In his *Demographic Factors in the Evolution of Nations*, Gini outlined the tenets of a population policy which he later helped to launch under fascism. He advocated radical eugenic remedies to restore the fecundity of the Italian race. Government, he declared, must implement a comprehensive pronatalist programme based on 'positive' incentives for fertility increase. Citizens must be given material rewards in the form of welfare benefits and tax breaks to induce them to fulfil their patriotic duty to procreate prolifically. Punitive measures must also be used to punish celibates and couples with few children and to redistribute the costs of reproduction more equitably. The entire machinery of the state, the legal system, the police and public institutions must be mobilized in order to put pressure on people to marry early and have large families (Quine 1990: 52–3).

Gini believed that a broad pronatalist and welfarist policy would succeed in engineering radical mutations in the reproductive habits of the Italian people in the space of one generation alone. This claim became the basis of fascism's fecundity drive in the interwar period. In 1927, Mussolini boasted optimistically that fascism would increase the population by almost twenty million to sixty million by 1950. He also explained that his demographic campaign aimed at achieving a *minimo di mortalità* (minimum mortality) and a *massimo di natalità* (maximum natality). The Duce wanted both quantity and quality. This apparently paradoxical goal was based on Gini's bizarre premise that fertile people were robust. Gini and his many disciples correlated high procreative output positively with a range of desirable racial traits, such as longevity and resistance to disease. He also attributed a number of symptoms of demographic degeneration, such as predisposition to alcoholism, tuberculosis, stillbirth and early death, to diminished sex drive (Quine 1990: 48–9 and 60–6). This connection between reproductive fitness and physical health explains why the fascist regime could later argue, seemingly so illogically, that if the birthrate were to rise, rates of mortality and morbidity would fall.

A fertility debate among economists also influenced fascist population policy. At the turn of the century, Achille Loria, a socialist economist, devised a fascinating neo-mercantilist theory of economic development based on a critique of Malthus. Loria argued that a fear of over-population was no longer justified in an industrial age.

Writing in an earlier era when productive constraints limited agricultural output, Malthus had believed that famine and misery were unavoidable. But modern economies, according to Loria, could comfortably accommodate the needs of growing populations (Quine 1990: 41–2).

Limits to food production in Italy, Loria contended, could easily be overcome by means of agrarian reform. He proposed that the state implement a policy aimed at redistributing property more evenly and alleviating landlessness among peasants. Public reclamation and irrigation projects to extend arable land would make the countryside better able to sustain population growth by means of the resettlement of families on farms. And crop yield, even on smallholdings, could be improved through more widespread use of machinery and chemicals. A revival of the rural economy, Loria believed, would halt mass emigration from regions where demographic pressures caused the jobless to flee. Improvements in agriculture would also have a knock-on effect for the economy as a whole. Enlarging peasant proprietorship would increase incomes, raise levels of consumption, strengthen the home market and generate demand for manufactured goods. A modernized Italian agriculture could positively contribute to the industrial expansion of an integrated and balanced national economy which would need ever more workers to sustain progress (Quine 1990: 43–6).

Italian pronatalism seemed to provide answers to some of Italy's most pressing problems as a poor nation. The arguments of economists like Loria undoubtedly convinced many that self-sufficiency in food production was possible, even though Italian agriculture was so backward. Importantly too, Loria and others depicted population increase as a precondition for a 'completion' of industrialization. In a book entitled *The Nightmare of Depopulation*, Georgio Mortara, one of Italy's most distinguished liberal economists, warned that economic regression would ensue should Italy's birthrate continue to decline. Other prewar theorists argued that Italy had to increase its supply of 'human capital' in order to compensate for the country's deficiencies in wealth and resources. A scarcity of labour, they warned, spelled disaster for the nation, as levels of unionization, militancy and wages increased as population declined (Quine 1990: 50). No more than mere 'numbers' as Mussolini would later echo, the prolific proletariat had become the raw material necessary to fuel economic development.

Pronatalist economists recognized that native industry was so uncompetitive and export-dependent that it remained vulnerable to trade fluctuations. Italian industry was hindered by a lack of capital for investment, as well as the high prices for essential raw materials for manufacture. Industrialization was an expensive proposition for a nation with so few natural resources. In this context, their goal of population increase in such a poor and populous country had a peculiar logic. Italy's disadvantaged position as a 'late industrializer' caused many to realize just where the nation's only competitive edge lay – in its inverterately low-waged economy. The one asset capitalists could rely on to produce profit was a chronically saturated labour market which resulted in depressed wages. The new pronatalism may have extolled the virtues of Italy's productive and prolific proletariat. But the rhetoric really amounted to little more than a willingness to sacrifice workers' welfare to the national interest. Any long-term rise in levels of population growth would obviously intensify already acute demographic pressures on family incomes and living standards. But the pronatalists' constant mention of the need to increase 'human capital' makes sense when labour is considered as a factor in production. Steady and sustained population growth would ensure that Italy could afford to develop by off-loading production costs on to poorly-paid workers. Pronatalists were in effect advocating that Italy continue to industrialize on the cheap.

To this economic imperative, pronatalists added military considerations. Corrado Gini, for example, felt threatened by the sheer numerical preponderance of the people of Tsarist Russia. Despite the expanse of Russia's natural frontiers, the imperial army was large enough to protect the empire from invasion. But the Italian kingdom was vulnerable to attack as a Continental power with inland and seaboard borders. Italy had to increase the size of its armed forces in order to protect national security. This theme of strength through numbers reappeared in Mussolini's pronouncements on population. In his famous Ascension Day Speech of 26 May 1927, the Duce argued that forty million Italians compared unfavourably with ninety million Germans and 200 million Slavs. France loomed as a mighty military power with a combined resident and colonial population of over 130 million, and the British ruled over a huge empire of over 500 million inhabitants (Quine 1990: 7).

The size of the armies that other nations could mobilize disquieted Italians whose nation seemed weak. This impulse to see population size as the most important determinant of national strength was echoed later in Mussolini's essay entitled 'Numbers as Force', which first appeared in print in 1928. The fall of great past civilizations, he argued, had always been preceded by a decline in the birthrate. Birthrate increase was a political priority since armed conflict between peoples was part of the natural order of things. Compared to the 'yellow' and 'black' races of Africa and the East, Italians were failing to reproduce in sufficient numbers to safeguard the future. Sometime in the future, destiny would call upon them to assert their overwhelming superiority over lesser races. The show of power and force was what world politics was all about, so Italy needed large numbers of men who were fit enough to wage war (Quine 1990: 8–9).

What Mussolini had in mind when he contemplated Italy's status as a future great power was the conquest of empire. Imperialist ambitions also lay behind many of the arguments of earlier pronatalists. During the liberal period, the frantic bid for empire became a matter of international prestige. Italian colonialism brought few economic rewards, but the longing for territorial acquisition deepened at a time when other nations had completed their expansionist drive. Contemporary observers recorded that Italy's East African campaign in Tripoli in 1911 was accompanied by an outburst of nationalist euphoria. An observer of these events, Roberto Michels, commented that possible economic gains from colonial possessions mattered little to his compatriots. Italians suffered from an inferiority complex. What really lay behind their imperialism, Michels believed, was an aggressive and defensive 'psychic need to create empire' (Quine 1990: 25).

The new pronatalism seemed to confirm this belief. Many of the most outspoken advocates of population increase were eugenicists and racists. One of the founders of eugenics, Achille Loria, contended that a 'white European' represented a 'social capital at least ten times superior to that of an Oriental'. That the 'yellow races' of the East should reproduce with such vigour was a threat to a Europe committing 'race suicide'. Carlo Francesco Ferraris argued that any nation which did not criminalize contraception and abortion was destined to become an impotent 'eunuch race'. A former socialist, Napoleone Colajanni, wrote *Latins and Anglo-Saxons: Inferior and Superior Races* in 1906, a work which fused Marxism with eugenics. Because of the obstacle of belated nationhood and industrialization, he asserted, the 'Italic race' could compete with great powers only by accelerating the pace of economic development. Even a liberal politician like Francesco Nitti declared 'Latin fecundity' to be a civilizing force which would inspire the rebirth of a second Roman empire. The revolutionary syndicalist, Paolo Orano, who later became a supporter of fascist race laws, called condoms a tool of international capital and a 'bourgeois conspiracy' to keep 'proletarian Italy' weak. National survival depended on whether future generations would produce enough workers and warriors to create a powerful New Italy. Pronatalism captured so much support and cut across traditional party loyalties because it sprang from a well of frustrated nationalist sentiment (Quine 1990: 21).

In his Ascension Day Speech on 26 May 1927, Mussolini defined the objectives of his regime, chief among which was the goal of population increase. He argued that a nation transformed by fascism could comfortably accommodate at least ten million more citizens. Reclamation projects to clear cultivable land and agrarian reforms to boost crop yields would make Italy self-sufficient in food production 'within ten years'. And a future empire would absorb any excess population in colonial settlements. In his 'Numbers as Force' essay, the Duce launched an attack against neo-Malthusianism which borrowed heavily from earlier eugenic pronatalists. He specifically addressed the question of subsistence when criticizing advocates of birth control. Population increase, he argued, would not cause unemployment to rise or famine to ensue. He claimed that one of the most troubling weaknesses of the Italian economy, chronic under-consumption, did not derive from low wages and living standards. On the contrary, a falling birthrate stunted the growth of a home market and manufacturing productivity. Italy, in fact, was underpopulated and needed more workers and consumers to accelerate economic expansion (Quine 1990: 8–9).

The demographic campaign was central to fascist rule in Italy. The 'battle for the birthrate' was tied to the larger foreign policy and political aims of fascism. Because it was launched by a fascist dictatorship, the Italian pronatalist programme must be understood within the context of the ideology and practice of Mussolini's regime.

Firstly, population policy under fascism served to mediate relations between state and society. Fascism governed by means of consent and coercion. On the one hand, Mussolini consolidated a repressive dictatorship which destroyed all trade union, political and civil liberties. But the regime also attempted to mobilize popular support by integrating the masses into a national community. When Mussolini became premier in 1922, the PNF (Partito Nazionale Fascista) had only 300,000 members and the presence of the party barely extended beyond the regions of Emilia-Romagna and Tuscany. By contrast, about 13,750,000 Germans voted for the Nazis in 1932 and about 849,000 belonged to the party in 1933 (Merkl 1980: 756).

Furthermore, the National Socialists came to power after almost a decade of struggle during which time they had strengthened their party by creating a nationwide network of cells and had built up an electoral following by mobilizing constituents. Italian fascism had only a very limited base of support when its leader formed his first government. After his assumption to the premiership, Mussolini actively courted the establishment and made peace with the Church, the monarchy, big industrialists and powerful landowners. But he had yet to gain the loyalty of the working class. Fascism created a new style of modern mass politics in which propaganda was used as an instrument of political persuasion.

Fascist propaganda had an overwhelming presence in daily life under the dictatorship as the state seized control of the machinery of mass communication, the press, newsreels and the radio. During the twenty-one years of fascist governance, the drive to increase the birthrate figured prominently in the regime's unstinting efforts to portray a positive image of itself as a strong state with a mission. Ordinary Italians faced a constant barrage of claims about the many achievements of the first government in Italy to be committed to the health and welfare of its people. The dictatorship also implemented an authoritarian plan to alter Italian fertility. The numerous legislative and institutional initiatives which accompanied the birthrate campaign gave the state much leverage for social control and marked the inauguration of public intervention in private life as a form of fascist rule.

Secondly, population policy also became an integral part of the political mythology surrounding a party in power which was otherwise bereft of a systematic doctrine and ideology. Fascism depended on the propagation of certain political myths to give it credence with the public. Chief among these was the myth of itself as a revolutionary movement which stood for the creation of a powerful New Italy (Cannistraro 1972: 116–17). What one historian has called fascism's 'palingenetic vision' became an indispensable instrument of dictatorial power (Griffin 1991: 32–6). To capture the consciousness of the people, the regime constructed an image of itself as the embodiment of a momentous 'national resurrection'. The fascist 'revolution' was a radical new beginning after a dark age of decline under liberalism. The language used in the dictatorship's pronatalist propaganda reflected fascism's claim to be a progressive and regenerative force in Italian politics. The Duce promised to 'heal, cure, and restore' a nation which had become 'sick, weak, and degenerate' under liberal parliamentary democracy. Mussolini's pronouncements on the birthrate included constant mention of a 'spiritual renewal' of the Italian people and the 'rebirth' of a 'young and fertile race'. The regime also presented its population policy as an ambitious form of social planning and engineering by a government determined to remake Italy into a proud, productive and prolific nation. As health reforms figured prominently in the demographic campaign, fascists spoke of a 'welfare revolution' which the caring and benevolent state had purportedly enacted.

Scholars have also recognized that through its myths, symbols, rituals and beliefs, fascism sought to make once-free citizens into loyal followers of a new political faith with mass-mobilizing ambitions. Some historians contend that fascism functioned as a 'secular religion' centred on the 'sacralization' of the state, the deification of the leader and the promulgation of a nationalist ideology which was taken to the point of mysticism (Gentile 1990: 229–51). By means of its populist and integrative policies, the regime attempted to 'nationalize' the masses by giving them a patriotic pride and a national identity (Mosse 1975: chs 1 and 9; De Grazia 1992: ch. 1). Fascism extolled the virtues and values of *Italianità*, the quality and essence of being Italian, chief among which was what was boastfully called 'hyper-fecundity'. Fascist pronatalism presented fertility and virility as attributes of a superior 'Italic race' which must be cherished and preserved. Pronatalist nationalism aimed to convince the Italian people that they shared a common destiny as bearers of a noble Roman civilization and creators of a New Fascist Imperium (Weber 1964: 18–19). Pronatalist ideology made reference to the glorious past and future of the race in order to legitimate the political objectives of the dictatorship.

Population policy also embodied many of the contradictory aims of the dictatorship. On the one hand, the birthrate campaign was linked in the official ideology with fascism's attempts to modernize the economy. The fascist corporate order needed more workers to build the motorways, FIAT cars, Olivetti typewriters and hydroelectric plants which were supposed to transform Italy from a second-rate capitalist power into an industrial giant. Fascism stood for all that was dynamic and innovative. In typical 1920s fashion, the regime celebrated modernity and claimed that it was a 'modernizing' dictatorship (Gregor 1974: 251–2; Turner 1975: 117–39). But, on the other hand, pronatalism provided the ideological mainstay of the dictatorship's ruralization programme. Projects to reclaim marshland for settlement by farmers, controls on immigration abroad and internal migration and increased police powers to banish vagrants and beggars to their village of origin were all part of a slowy attempt to 'depopulate' major cities. Fascist ruralism had a decidedly anti-modernist tone. The urban world was equated with the vices of individualism, consumerism and feminism which had allegedly caused the birthrate to decline. Fascism extolled the virtues of a fecund rural Italy and promised to support the peasant proprietor and leaseholder.

Fascist peasantism, though, appeared to be no more than an ideological artifice to divert attention away from a crisis in the countryside. The paradox is that despite its ruralist rhetoric, fascism presided over Italy's transition from a predominantly agricultural into a mature industrial economy (Corner 1979: 239–74). During and after the depression, rural unemployment rose markedly and the size of the agricultural work force shrank. Land ownership and cultivation also changed dramatically. Increasing fragmentation of holdings undermined the viability of the peasant household economy by making it difficult for families to feed themselves from minute plots. Labour and tenancy agreements became more harsh as landlords chose to maintain profits by cutting wages and increasing rents. As prices for their products plummeted, many smallholders accumulated debts and lost farms to creditors. These processes encouraged rural flight and undermined efforts to halt *bracciantizzazione* (proletarianization of agricultural labour). Far from protecting rural Italy from economic adversity, the fascist regime's policies consistently favoured industry over agriculture (Cohen 1979: 70–87; Corner 1993: 51–68). While the dictatorship actively sought to encourage recovery in industrial production, it did little to salvage the agricultural sector.

The contradictions within fascist population policy are also evident in the timing of the launch of the demographic campaign. Mussolini officially inaugurated the 'battle for births' when a grave currency crisis hit the Italian economy. Losing ground after 1924, the lira collapsed on the world market in 1927. For reasons of political prestige, the Duce moved quickly to prop up the weak lira abroad. *Quota novanta*, or revaluation on the parity of ninety to the pound, squeezed liquidity and brought on recession at home (Welk 1938: 164–76; Sarti 1970: 97–112). Mass unemployment ensued. However, with trade unions domesticated and the strike weapon banned, labour had no say in determining the wages and conditions of work. The state had helped big industry to consolidate its control over workers through the Pact of Palazzo Vidoni, concluded on 2 October 1925, and employers pugnaciously wielded their power over those on the payroll. Management had free reign to enforce public policy in drastic, across-the-board wage reductions, but they also extended repressive tactics in unofficial cost-saving measures. Workers bore the brunt of maintaining production and decreasing expenditure. They were fired, then rehired at reduced rates, while part-time scheduling replaced standard full and overtime practice. Thus even before the Wall Street crash of 1929, underemployment and unemployment became structural realities of the Italian economy. The start of recovery after 1929 varied from one sector to another, but the economy as a whole awakened from depression only when the regime prepared for a succession of expansionist pushes after 1932 by implementing autarky, a form of economic nationalism which some historians believe created a 'permanent war economy'. Fascist economic policy followed the dictates of foreign policy as wars in Ethiopia, Spain and Albania between 1935 and 1939 stimulated manufacturing in heavy industries.

What distinguished fascist economic policy, then, was that it relied upon high unemployment, a drastic reduction of private consumption, deteriorating living standards and the powerlessness of the working class. Relegated to the least desirable and lowest paid work in old and new textile industries and the traditional sweated trades, women, moreover, held a particularly disadvantaged position within the work force which fascism only served to accentuate. Levels of wages, regular employment and job opportunities for females were low in Italy compared to those of other countries. Because of the backwardness of the economy, the mass entry of women into better paid white-collar positions which happened in Germany after the First World War did not occur in interwar Italy. Although it hesitated to impose the kind of formal legal quotas on women's work which the Nazi regime implemented between 1933 and 1936, the Italian dictatorship allowed industrialists to restructure the female labour market by means of unofficial exclusionary measures (Mason, 1976: 74–113 and 5–31; Noether 1982: 72–4). Female factory labourers under fascism became younger as married women were simply shunted out of the work force. Despite these harsh economic realities which reduced the incomes and security of families, fascism saw fit to launch an aggressive policy aimed at increasing the birthrate.

The demographic campaign was a battle on many fronts which legitimated active public interventionism in the private sphere. Fascism was quick to recognize that the family could be used as an instrument of political rule. The notion of a Fascist Family of loyal followers gained currency in government propaganda. This idea reflected the dictatorship's 'totalitarian' aspiration to inculcate new values and beliefs in parents and children, integrate all Italians in family life, influence private behaviour and extend power over the domestic domain. State interference in the arena of personal life, however, challenged the control that the Catholic Church still wielded over reproduction, socialization and welfare.

The model of a Fascist Family was a direct challenge to the Church's doctrine of the Christian Family. The Vatican understood that the dictatorship's pronatalist programme politicized the functions of marriage, the family and procreation. In December 1930, Pope Pius XI issued Christian Marriage, an encyclical which spoke of the sacramental nature of wedlock. Christian parents should understand, he warned, that they were to 'bear offspring for the Church of Christ, to procreate saints and servants of God' (Noonan 1966: 426). Christians should worship their saviour by having large families, but they should not propagate plentifully in order to satisfy the objectives of the state. Only the Vatican had the right to lay down divine law on the goals of matrimony and the duties of Catholics. The papacy again reacted to fascist encroachments on its exclusive and higher authority over these matters when in May 1931 another encyclical criticized the welfare policies of Mussolini's regime. As part of its plan to give people material incentives to increase fertility, the fascist state sought to secularize the system of ecclesiastical and voluntary associations ministering to the poor and the sick. The attempt to consolidate a modern welfare state by integrating all existing institutions into a new national health service threatened Church and lay Catholic control over charity. In 1931, the Pope reaffirmed the principle that all assistance to needy families should strengthen the 'moral order' by having a redemptive rather than a political purpose (Quine 1990: 241).

Despite these injunctions, fascism continued to penetrate and mobilize the private sphere. The demographic campaign inspired major changes in the law, perhaps the most famous of which was the regime's decision in December 1926 to impose a bachelor tax on unmarried men. As in other policy areas, fascism looked to Italy's imperial past to justify this initiative. The regime presented its 'celibacy tax' as a direct borrowing from the golden age of Emperor Augustus in Late Antiquity. The Roman precedent aside, the celibacy tax ostensibly aimed at providing an inducement to marriage and at redistributing national income towards large families. Immediate inspiration for this 'negative' measure derived from France where in 1920 the legislature made single men and women, as well as married couples with no children, pay an additional contribution from income tax. Financial motives also influenced this ploy to exact revenue for the deeply indebted Italian state. Only priests and soldiers were exempt from payment, while the aged, the indigent and the sick had to apply for special dispensation. Calculated on the basis of age and income, the celibacy tax hit some categories especially hard. For unmarried men between the ages of 35 and 50, it amounted to a 25 per cent surcharge on income tax and an additional flat rate of fifty lire a year. The government regularly raised rates and fines for evasion, so between 1927 and 1934, the amount collected trebled. Initially, the state channelled this money into social spending on welfare, but in 1935 it diverted these funds into the African campaign and afterwards used them to reduce the Treasury's chronic budget deficit (Glass 1967: 237).

Although they proved to be unsuccessful, punitive fiscal measures to boost the birthrate were an essential part of fascism's population policy. The government repeatedly threatened to impose even harsher penalties against 'premeditated sterility'. Party officials talked about banning single people over 30, childless couples and parents with fewer than four children from relatively well-paid and secure jobs in the public sector. They also seriously considered introducing a hefty 'infecundity tax' on the income of married persons with few children. They discussed too whether the state should appropriate the property of deceased people with no direct heirs and the inherited wealth of single people. And absurdly, Mussolini's closest advisers recommended that celibacy be 'criminalized' so that all citizens over 30 would be legally compelled to marry and produce offspring. Another possibility was to empower courts to annul marriages which remained childless after five years. Some even wished to make childlessness a crime against the state and the race which was punishable by a prison sentence and hefty fines (Quine 1990: 247–8).

Pronatalism gave a semblance of purpose to all policy initiatives under fascism. Fascism fought hard to redefine the exercise of citizenship and to make procreation appear to be a patriotic duty. The state accorded the nation's most prolific special privileges and a favoured status. Following the example of similar legislation introduced in France in 1914, the dictatorship gave tax breaks to fathers in 1928. As in France, spokesmen welcomed these changes by mention of the need for a system of 'redistributive justice' to alleviate the economic pressures on men who had to support many dependents. Advocates spoke of the plight of parents who were impoverished by high taxes and childcare costs while single people selfishly enjoyed large disposable incomes. In theory, male heads of households could now claim substantial reductions in income, property and local and provincial government taxes, as well as exemption from school and other taxes. But the reality did not live up to the hype lavished on this measure. In order to qualify, employees in the public sector or armed forces had to have at least seven dependents living at home; and workers in private industry had to have at least ten (Glass 1967: 238–9). Even in a Catholic country like Italy, those who actually met these eligibility requirements were a small minority of the total population.

Fascism preferred great shows of public support for families to more costly forms of social welfare. Always accompanied by propaganda blitzes, a whole series of initiatives seemed to mark a commitment by government to protect Italian mothers. In 1932, the regime created the *Giornata della Madre e del Fanciullo* (Mother's and Child's Day), a national holiday to be celebrated annually on Christmas eve. After the creation of empire in 1936, the state sponsored nationwide competitions for the title of 'Prolific Mother of the Year'. In addition to commemorative medals of honour, winners received *premi di natalità*, small gifts of cash. These birth premiums were scaled according to reproductive output, with fifty lire given for each child up to the sixth, one hundred lire for each child up to the tenth and two hundred for each child up to the twentieth. Fascist officials also dispensed special *premi di nuptialità* to newly-wed women who had produced a child annually during the first five years of their marriage (Quine 1990: 129–30).

Fascism also moved quickly to implement a broad policy of social hygiene as part of its demographic campaign. This initiative resulted partly from the desire to eradicate forms of illness which adversely affected levels of fertility and mortality. Begun in 1923, the 'battle against tuberculosis' reached fever pitch in a state-controlled media which exaggerated the accomplishments of the regime's measures for disease control. Most memorable among these was a law of December 1923 which extended the statutory provision already outlined by an act of July 1919. The 1919 legislation had established the famous 'Childrens' Colonies' for which fascism subsequently took the credit. The dictatorship made much of the fact that thousands of youngsters deemed to be predisposed to tuberculosis were entitled to free summer holidays in mountain, forest and beach resorts where they took the 'fresh air and food cure' pioneered by the new 'fascist sciences' of nutrition and puericulture. And because of the benevolence of government under fascism, children suffering from the sickness were sent to state-run rest homes where they received the latest 'solarium' treatments.

Officials argued that the fascist 'welfare revolution' would safeguard the 'physical integrity of the race'. Fascism promised to rationalize public health provision, professionalize science and medicine and modernize medical education and care. The first of its kind in Italy, the fascist programme of social hygiene gave some credence to the regime's claim to be a government committed to 'collectivized medicine', a phrase used repeatedly by loyalists. In 1923, a long overdue 'reorganization of public administration' paved the way for fascist reforms by increasing the burden on provincial and municipal authorities to provide a full range of health services, including an Office of Hygiene in all communes with more than 20,000 inhabitants. From 1925, when the state launched an initiative to increase the number of public health facilities, party officials presided over the openings of sanatoria throughout the kingdom. However, private donations, rather than state funding, paid for the construction of these and many other new welfare institutions under fascism.

While the dictatorship hesitated to increase substantially state spending on welfare, fascism created a social climate which promoted private philanthropy and public health awareness. In 1928, the regime welcomed the establishment of the nation's first professorship in tuberculosis and respiratory disease at Rome's Royal University. National guidelines encouraged agencies like the Italian Red Cross to cooperate with government authorities and party organizations in order to mount a nationwide educational campaign and to raise money for free clinics where people could be tested for disease. And a decree issued in 1928 approved the provision of 'tuberculosis insurance' for those categories of workers who already contributed, along with their employers, to a sickness benefit scheme. At least in theory, the act expanded statutory health coverage by giving those who qualified, along with their families, free hospitalization for an indefinite period and financial indemnity for the loss of income. But the political motivation behind these reforms cannot be ignored. In fascist Italy, welfare and propaganda were interlocked. And just as importantly, the dictatorship's actual achievements seldom matched the inflated claims made by government.

Fascism's social aspiration may have been to improve all areas of public provision for the health and welfare of the rural and urban working classes. But since the obstacles to social development in

Italy were great, so many of the regime's policy targets went unrealized. Some of the reasons for this failure were beyond the control of the fascist government. Liberalism had bequeathed to fascism a weak economy and a fragile state unable to create the prosperity and progress which the nineteenth century had promised. The values of industrial capitalism and the drive to 'national efficiency and fitness' had inspired fascism's predecessors to seek to make some rudimentary improvements in housing, sanitation, nutrition, medicine and employment. But for all the efforts of liberal leaders, only a bare foundation of the 'welfare state' had been built by the time Mussolini came to power. Rather than causing a complete break from established tradition, fascism continued the social mission of liberal statecraft. The regime expanded the protective legislation it had inherited from previous administrations and integrated new laws into an explicit programme for social hygiene and population growth.

However, the legislative fever which overcame reform-minded fascist planners was without precedent. As part of its policy of preventive social medicine, for example, the fascist state issued scores of amendments to already existing laws governing the control and treatment of malaria, a major killer in low-lying areas throughout the country. Fascism undoubtedly had the political will to combat the spread of a disease which posed a threat to the nation's health. But the economic resources which it directed at public health reform were far too limited to merit the claim that fascism had nationalized medicine and built a 'welfare state'. Government had to do more than just put an endless stream of ambitious and far-reaching legislation on the books. One historical lesson learned from fascist over-ambition was that the real test of social policy is not its aims, however commendable, but rather whether the state can actually implement reforms effectively. The reality was that fascism failed in its resolve to create a 'New Order' in which the right of the poor to enjoy good health was safeguarded by a protective and caring state.

Just one instance of where the best intentions were not good enough was when the fascist government set ever more stringent guidelines regulating the working conditions of labourers who were particularly at risk of malarial infection. The rice workers of Piedmont had long been recognized to be vulnerable to all sorts of respiratory and infectious diseases, such as tuberculosis, bronchitis and malaria. Throughout the wetlands of the north-west, rice workers slept on hay strewn over dirt floors in sheds without running water, ventilation or electricity. These migrant workers also toiled for long hours in paddy-fields for low wages and little food. The regime aimed to introduce improvements by making it compulsory for employers to provide decent housing and better medical care. But the health visits and proper amenities promised by fascism did not materialize, for the simple reason that the big agrarians who owned the rice farms had absolutely no incentive or compulsion to sacrifice profits for the welfare of their work force. The type of enlightened entrepreneurship that the dictatorship envisaged would never come about as long as employers could get away with paying and treating their workers badly (Quine 1990: ch. 6).

What the 'battle against malaria' reveals is that fascism legislated, but did not implement, many of Italy's most needed reforms. The regime simply chose not to enforce the bulk of its social hygiene policies affecting workers' health. The body of laws which fascism created was so impressive in size and substance that it gave the impression that the regime actually transformed the historically weak Italian state and its minimal social policy into a new kind of activist governance. But the aggressive style of state interventionism and public welfarism which the dictatorship espoused was no more than mere rhetoric. This was most evident in the regime's daring moves to 'safeguard the morality of the race'. As an accompaniment to the public health programme, the government introduced a whole series of legislation aimed at 'moral hygiene'. What new enactments seemed to promise was a complete break with tradition by a dictatorship determined to extend state control over private life.

Beginning in 1923, the regime's 'battle against alcoholism' resulted in numerous statutes regulating the alcohol content, production, sale and distribution of wine and spirits. Other repressive acts making drunkenness in public places a 'crime against the race' increased the severity of permissible punishments, including fine and imprisonment. The state may have succeeded in prohibiting a new generation of schoolchildren from enjoying a glass of water and wine at lunch, as their parents and grandparents had done before them, but it certainly did not manage to prevent the numerous reported illegalities in wine production. Similarly, fascist planners launched a campaign in 1923 to combat the trafficking of drugs like cocaine and opium, whose use for other than medical reasons was already illegal. Police were meant to mobilize all resources in the war against drugs, but the number of charges brought and of convictions secured for drug-related offences did not rise during the fascist period. Fascism had little real success in its attempts to fight the 'social diseases' like drug and alcohol abuse which purportedly endangered the health of the race.

The regime made a more serious effort to combat venereal disease, which medical experts believed increased the incidence of mental illness, infant mortality and infertility. But even this health campaign had a limited scope as almost all initiatives were aimed at sexual regulation. Targeting women as carriers of contagion, the state sought to limit the spread of syphilis by restricting prostitution to registered houses. Local government enlisted more doctors to examine prostitutes and issue them with health certificates. Beginning in 1923, public order laws expanded police powers to arrest and detain suspected prostitutes. The regime accompanied these attempts at the surveillance of streetwalking by a drive to stop so-called 'white slavery'.

The belief that agents working for an organized network of sex merchants picked up young village women at railway stations and then sold them into slavery was very widespread. Parliament debated the issue and set out to protect the nation's innocents from the traffic in flesh allegedly carried out by an international syndicate. But all the fuss amounted to little more than repeated injunctions to the police to be more vigilant when patrolling the streets. In its new penal code of 1930, the regime neither made the so-called 'corruption of minors' a felony nor did it harshen penalties against this misdemeanour. The number of men charged with being pimps increased annually during the fascist period, though most offenders walked free after paying a fine. The number of under-age women who were taken in by the police for questioning also increased annually, but the system worked differently for them. Authorities concerned about the morality of the young sent them to be 're-educated' by the many private and Church charities for wayward girls (Quine 1990: ch. 9).

'Moral hygiene' involved a whole set of attitudes about 'normal' and 'deviant' sexual practice and social behaviour. So intimately connected with fascism's self-image as a moralizing force upholding healthy traditional values, 'moral hygiene' permeated many areas of social policy during the dictatorship. Some of these, like the 'battle against pornography', were frenzied attempts by the state to restrict the boundaries of sexuality. From 1927, the regime ordered the *carabinieri* to sequester foreign books and magazines showing nudity, which was deemed to be offensive to public morals. Included among the list of illegal 'pornographic' material were sex toys and contraceptive devices, excluding the condom, as well as manuals dealing with such forbidden subjects as birth control. Police turned a blind eye to literature aimed at teenagers on the 'evils' of mastur- bation and promiscuity because these had an 'educational' and 'redemptive' purpose. Fascism also stood up as the moral guardian of young boys whose psycho-sexual development could be damaged by comic books and adventure stories. Attempts to control the commerce in boys' fiction were especially energetic, as these were tied to the regime's 'campaign against juvenile delinquency'.

Policy makers listened to medical experts who believed that modern 'heroic' literature caused 'sexual excitation' before puberty and predisposed boys to criminality. Youngsters from deprived back- grounds were especially prone to crime because of their family history, so they had to be watched carefully for any noticeable signs of 'anti-social' tendencies. Inspired by eugenic ideas about the inheritability of illness, the regime's programme for 'moral hygiene' wilfully crossed over into the territory of 'mental hygiene'. The fascist police used their increased powers to put 'suspicious' youths into protective custody. Even homeless children who had committed no crime were picked up off the streets and sent to institutions for intelligence and psychological testing (Quine 1990: ch. 9). Other significant 'social diseases', such as homosexuality and even swear- ing, received considerable attention by the fascist state. Denounced as a corrupting influence on the young, bad language was discour- aged by the regime's spokesmen and citizens were told to report offences to the police. Naturally enough, the dictatorship's 'battle against obscene speech' had as much to do with political repression as moral censure. Many allegations involved citizens making dirty and demeaning jokes about the baldness and fatness of Mussolini. The public did not fail to notice that their new Caesar did not live up to the official image of the Duce as a young and virile specimen of Italian manhood. Fairly tolerated by the state if not by social custom, homosexuality came under particular scrutiny only when criminal acts against minors were committed. As child abuse was not recognized legally, the police regularly charged molesters, flash- ers and rapists with 'corruption' or the lesser offence of 'indecent behaviour'. But the accused seldom faced trial.

One such case involved a 21-year-old male swimming instructor at a beach camp run by the regime's youth organization, the *Balilla*. When exposed by parents, the man confessed to his crimes, which included molesting a number of little boys, and he was charged with indecent behaviour. But under pressure from local fascist officials, and even Mussolini who was immediately notified, the case did not proceed to court because of extenuating circumstances. The instructor was a member and representative of the party, so his behaviour reflected badly on the regime. And politics aside, the authorities were agreed that he should be given another chance as even a short prison term could ruin the life of someone so young and impressionable. The actual legal technicality which saw his release was that since the acts were committed in 'private' they did not constitute an impermissible 'public' offence. A dictatorship so outwardly determined to protect future generations by stamping out varieties of 'sexual deviance' was none the less prepared to tolerate crimes against children in order to avoid scandal.

In its public pronouncements alone, the regime appeared to be more protective towards women and children than previous governments had been. A central part of the demographic campaign involved the launch of a major initiative to improve medical and social services for mothers and babies. The creation of ONMI, the *Opera Nazionale per la Protezione della Maternità ed Infanzia* (the National Organization for the Protection of Motherhood and Infancy) in 1925 seemed to herald a new style of Italian welfarism devoted to improving and extending the public provision of care. The regime called the new institution a fine example of fascism's commitment to a 'welfare revolution' in a country where the Church and private charities still controlled so much of the system of social assistance. Fascism could be proud of its legislative achievement, for the founding statutes of ONMI promised to build clinics and nurseries, to open soup kitchens and milk dispensaries, to mobilize a young generation of doctors and social workers to care for the people, and to educate the public about health and nutrition. But once again, fascism proved to be overly ambitious in its plans for a 'New Order'.

The actual impact of fascist welfare reforms was minimal since the state hesitated to fund ONMI's many initiatives generously. Outside big cities, ONMI's presence remained limited to periodic philanthropic drives and propaganda campaigns designed to depict the dictatorship in a favourable light. The much celebrated 'clinics' seldom provided real medical care and worked instead as centres where women picked up booklets on how to be a good mother. The actual number of institutions catering to women and children did increase under fascism. But much of the 'care' they received was in the form of one-off hand-outs of baby clothes, food and powdered milk rather than improved medical treatment and direct financial benefits. The social need for the national health service which ONMI might have become was indeed great. But the regime never maintained the momentum of reform, so the material standing of poor urban and rural women under fascism did not improve (Quine 1990: chs 4–5).

The basic assumption behind fascist pronatalism was that positive improvements to the conditions of the working class would convince Italians to have more babies. This social experiment was an ambitious undertaking for any state since there was no hard evidence that even an efficient welfare system could deliver material rewards substantial enough to influence the birthrate. In 1938, the regime begrudgingly pronounced the demographic campaign a complete failure, since the birth and marriage rates had continued to fall throughout what was to have been Italy's most 'fecund decade'. That the national level of mortality among first-years was higher in 1937 than it had been in 1927 also proved especially embarrassing for a regime committed to saving the lives of infants.

Whatever the odds against any population policy actually altering long-term demographic trends, it can be said with certainty that the fascist 'welfare state' offered women few real incentives to increase their fertility. This is partly because the regime did not champion the cause of all women but only that of mothers. Population policy embodied the ambivalent attitude of fascism towards women. The regime was overtly hostile to women's right to equality in public and private, and yet promised to protect all of Italy's 'mothers of the race'. Fascism did accentuate the discrimination Italian women already faced in politics, education, the law, the economy and the family. The dictatorship justified this assault against women's advancement by repeated mention of the so-called 'natural hierarchy' between the sexes. Fascism's militarist ethos held 'heroic', 'masculine' values in high regard. Even pronatalist ideology had a masculinist slant in that the official line always described the Italian race in such terms as 'noble', 'warrior' and 'virile'. In the fascist version of biological sex difference, men were assigned a role as fearless front-line soldiers who took to battle to defend 'eternal Rome' while women fulfilled their own allotted mission by staying at home, having babies and sacrificing their sons for the nation.

This image of the housebound mother was never more than a myth since millions of working women juggled family responsibilities with underpaid, unprotected and often seasonal jobs in textile factories, the clothing and furnishing trades, food and service industries and in agriculture. Because of the failure of its economic policies, the regime never delivered to workers the decent 'living wage' promised in the 1926 Labour Charter. Nor did fascism take seriously its commitment to improve the conditions of women in regular but undervalued employment or in all kinds of 'invisible' and exploited domestic manufacture. Not only were women wage-earners in fascist Italy, but also many of them were listed in censuses as primary 'heads-of-household', so their relative poverty had a direct impact on the incomes of families. In short, working-class living standards and quality of life remained low during the dictatorship. And because of that, to bear and rear healthy children was well beyond the reach of even the most selfless 'mothers of the nation' (Quine 1990: 112).

However progressive in aspiration fascist welfarism was in some respects, it was still predicated on the denial of reproductive rights and choices to Italian women. Decriminalization of abortion may have been unthinkable in interwar Italy whether or not the country was under a fascist dictatorship. But beginning in 1926, the regime did increase the severity of punishments and intensify the policing of citizens. The women ruled by fascism, however, have left a poignant reminder of their refusal to become mere 'reproducers of the race'. On 18 April 1928, police arrested a doctor in private practice in a small textile town outside Milan with a large working-class population. A house search uncovered the paraphernalia of an abortionist, as well as two jars of fully-formed foetuses. Payment receipts found in the doctor's surgery contained the names of four women who were subsequently brought in for interrogation. All four admitted to having procured an abortion for a sum roughly equivalent to a month's wage in factory work. Two of the women had decided to seek terminations because they were unmarried, while the remaining two did not wish to have any more children. Subsequent investigations revealed that at least one other married woman had recently died in hospital as a result of a botched abortion performed by the same doctor. The four women were fined heavily for their crimes but released from custody in order to avoid the risk of a public outcry. The police imposed additional fines on two of them because they did not cooperate while being detained.

A few days later, a group of angry women arrived at the town hall demanding the immediate release of the town's abortionist. The police arrived at the scene and forcibly disbanded the crowd. But by that evening, over a hundred women had joined the protest and were holding an all-night vigil outside police headquarters where the doctor was being held. They carried flowers, sang songs and waited peaceably. Officers arrested eight of the women on disorder offences and dispersed the rest. What the police described as a 'phenomenon of collective female solidarity' continued throughout the following two weeks. Finally, on 5 May, the police decided to release the doctor on condition that he leave town under their escort (Quine 1990: 112–13). We are left wondering what became of the women in the aftermath of their quiet siege, an organized and courageous act of outrage against a system which restricted their personal freedoms. This short episode in the history of the dictatorship is a strong reflection of what some women at least really wanted from the state.

2 Fathers of the nation
French pronatalism during the Third
Republic

Every man has the duty to contribute to the perpetuation of his
country exactly as he is bound to defend it.

> (M. Jacques Bertillon, chief statistician for the City of Paris and
> founding member of the National Alliance for the Increase of the
> French Population. From his address to the Extra-Parliamentary
> Commission on Depopulation, July 1902)

[It] is in fact upon the fathers of families that the birthrate of
the country depends.

> (Lucien March, director of the National Bureau of Statistics and
> founding member of the French Eugenics Society. From a paper
> delivered at the Second International Eugenics Conference,
> New York, 1921)

The French have long been sensitive to the slightest shifts in fertility.
For several centuries, political leaders and educated élites have perceived France's military prowess and economic power in sheer
numerical terms. Changes in population size have caused recurring
anxiety about national grandeur and decline. As early as the four-
teenth and fifteenth centuries, French governments sought to combat
underpopulation by enacting laws which encouraged marriage. Much
later, mercantilists avidly believed that demographic growth would
stimulate manufacture and trade. Louis XIV's finance minister, Jean
Baptiste Colbert, drafted legislation which took inspiration from
the population policies of Augustus and Caesar. Based on Roman
principles, his edict of 1666 not only prohibited emigration outside
the colonies but also entitled fathers of at least ten children to
exemptions for life from all taxes and generous old-age pensions
(Glass 1967: 91–2). During the late eighteenth century and the
Revolutionary period, various measures to discourage celibacy were
publicly discussed. These included proposals to ban single men from
public office, to require them to wear distinguishing dress and to

compel them to pay more taxes. Some also wished to make celibacy a capital offence (Ogden and Huss 1982: 287). In the early 1800s, pronatalist ideas dwindled somewhat as acceptance of Malthus' warnings about over-population spread. But by the middle of the nineteenth century, decades of birthrate decrease renewed fears of impending depopulation. After censuses revealed that for the first time the total number of deaths exceeded the number of births in the years 1854 and 1855, dire predictions of the nation's imminent demise abounded.

A barrage of alarmist literature appeared which portrayed France as a moribund nation suffering from the symptoms of demographic decline. In 1849, Raudot published his *On the Decadence of France*, a work motivated by the same preoccupations with natality which provoked Italians to write of national degeneration. The following decades saw the flourishing of nationalist accounts of how France would lose its position as a dominant Continental power if the birthrate were to continue to descend. Louis Napoleon's defeat by Bismarck in 1870–1, the consequent loss of territory to Prussia and the collapse of the Second Empire deepened the widespread belief that huge nations like Germany and Russia preponderated over France. By the end of the 1870s, pronatalist nationalism pervaded French society and dominated political life to an extent which was unparalleled in other countries. The nation with the longest history of fertility decline in all of modern Europe also produced the largest population movement, one comprised of a multitude of family and pronatalist interest groups with mass-mobilizing aims.

Despite the existence of a seeming pronatalist consensus in French politics during the Third Republic (1870–1945), successive governments implemented only discrete measures for birthrate increase rather than a systematic policy. French population policy developed incrementally over a number of years through gradual and piecemeal legislation. Not until 1939 did political leaders launch a comprehensive programme which enshrined these existing and new reforms in the *Code de la famille* (Family Code). Another distinguishing feature of French approaches to the 'population question', pronatalism gave rise to an evolving family policy whose goals were to give preferential treatment and economic benefits to those with three or more children. In contrast to Italian population policy, which, at least in theory, was based on a broad welfarist agenda according social rights to the whole of the working class, French initiatives were selectively targeted at only the nation's most prolific, regardless of class or income. Child allowances and a welter of other

forms of financial aid for *familles nombreuses* (big families) became
the pivot of French population policy. By the 1950s, France could
boast of being one of Europe's most generous providers of welfare
directed at families.

The French style of population policy sought to provide an assortment of 'positive' incentives for fertility increase which lent substantial support to families. A family-based scheme such as this was
limited in scope and discriminatory in the delivery of state welfare
since it was predicated on the principle that only large families
should be given special social rights. The remarks cited at the beginning of this chapter underline another peculiarity of pronatalist
debates and policies in France. Advocates of demographic growth
like Bertillon and March focused their appeal on fellow Frenchmen,
whom they implored to marry young and father at least three
children. Both French and Italian population policies were gender-
based. But while Italian fascist ideology elevated the status of
mothers and sought to edify maternity in propaganda and policies
aimed at women, French pronatalism exalted paternity and determined to favour fathers with privilege and reward.

The fascist 'welfare state' gave central place to the notion of the
reciprocal rights and responsibilities of individuals and the state.
Mussolini's dictatorship was the first government in unified Italy to
acknowledge that women needed substantial social support for the
bearing and rearing of children. In rewarding mothers for performing their patriotic service to the nation, the regime attempted to
implement a comprehensive reform package which was targeted
primarily at women. The regime did not do so out of any commitment to improve the position of women in Italian society. Fascist
'maternalism', the official ideology and policy extolling motherhood,
addressed women as mothers, but disregarded women's other roles
as workers and citizens. But by posing as the champion of the rights
of mothers of the race, the regime astutely recognized the central-
ity of childbirth in women's lives and cynically used maternalist
rhetoric as an instrument of political rule and ambition. Curiously,
French populationist rhetoric largely ignored the fact that it was,
after all, women who produced, or failed to produce in sufficient
numbers, the workers and warriors on which the nation's future
seemed to depend. French pronatalism undervalued the contribution
of women to the social order and saw them as a threat to the race
since they practised birth control. Many of those proposed measures
aimed specifically at women were punitive and repressive in nature,
such as tightened controls on abortion and contraception. French

pronatalism spoke mainly to male *chefs de famille* (heads of household) and conveyed the message that procreation was a political duty, much like military service, which *men* had to perform for the sake of the grandeur and prosperity of the *patrie*. Pronatalist ideas in France focused on paternity rights and this definite masculinist bent promoted reforms that mostly benefited men.

In France, pronatalist ideas from a number of diverse sources, such as utopian socialism and *laissez-faire* liberalism, can be traced back over the centuries. But by far the most important stimulus to the organized pronatalisms which arose after 1870 came from Frédéric Le Play (1806–82), a sociologist, engineer and traveller who formed a circle of disciples around the *Société d'économie sociale* (Society of Social Economy) and the journal, *La Réforme sociale*. Le Play had a huge and lasting influence on the development of what I will call 'familism', a pronatalist ideology advocating that families be given special social, economic and citizen rights. While other nations produced pro-family movements, the prevalence, impact and scope of French familism was both remarkable and unique. Familism can be found not only in the ideas of Le Play's followers who were social Catholics, but also in the programmes of later republican reformists, such as Bertillon (see p. 64–5). Although he may not even have been a practising Catholic, Le Play was a moralist who upheld that religious and family values were the cornerstones of a stable social order (Zeldin 1977: 955). In works such as his *Organization of the Family* (1871), Le Play outlined his utopian vision, one that was deeply reactionary and anti-modernist.

Le Play was a high priest and a precursor of a peculiarly French politics of reaction to modernity which became increasingly pervasive within the culture during the Third Republic. In his 1871 work, he harked back to an imagined idyllic past when paternal authority went unchallenged and social peace reigned. He described the 'patriarchal family' of traditional and rural societies as his ideal. The preindustrial social order, he declared, was founded on the household economy of the extended peasant family which had an investment in high fertility since everyone worked for the good of their collective security. Of the different types of inheritance for large holdings, Le Play favoured a system of primogeniture which kept patrimony intact. For this reason, he especially admired the English and Russian aristocracies of the eighteenth century who bequeathed the whole of their ancestral estates to their first-born sons (Le Play 1871: 8–9).

France, he believed, was a nation in which the rural order was threatened with extinction. In the countryside, small family plots increasingly dwindled in size with each succeeding generation. The revolution of 1789, Le Play argued, began a process of decline which hastened the disappearance of the large families of the *ancien régime* and the rise of the two-child families of the nineteenth century. By imposing laws for *partage forcé* which required that land be divided equally among all male and female, as well as legitimate and illegitimate, heirs, revolutionary leaders had endangered the moral and social fabric of France (Talmy, vol. 1, 1962: 41–2).

Equal division of property among all surviving children threatened the livelihood of families dependent on the land, encouraged rural flight and provided a compelling economic incentive for birth control. Industrialization and urbanization further undermined the institution of the family by fostering the spread of corrupting influences such as individualism, socialism and feminism. Modern societies were based on a new unstable 'nuclear family' in which cross-generational ties were fragile, paternal authority was weakened, fixed gender roles were relaxed and family wealth was dispersed. Not content to be a mere critic, Le Play used his journal to launch a campaign for social reform.

He advocated that French law recognize the importance of the family to the maintenance of social order. Believing that inheritance laws were the prime cause of birthrate decline in rural departments, Le Play wished to change the system of *partage* by depriving children of their automatic rights to a portion of the patrimony. In order to enjoy a decent standard of living and to preserve family wealth for future generations, peasant proprietors needed to limit the number of their offspring. Le Play aimed to remove this economic obstacle to population growth by reducing succession duties and empowering fathers to pick a principal heir. Greater testamentary freedom, he argued, would enhance paternal authority, ensure each generation had a *paterfamilias*, restore women to their primary reproductive roles and strengthen the 'natural' hierarchy within the family (Brooke 1970: 107). Since only the most capable son would be able to inherit the land, offspring would have to compete among themselves to win favour from their father. These authoritarian domestic arrangements, Le Play contended, would revive French agriculture by consolidating the bases of a class of prosperous peasant landowners.

Le Play had an enormous influence on politics during the Third Republic because he developed a reformist agenda about the ordinary domestic issues, such as the cost of raising children, which affected the living standards of much of the population. In an age when central government neglected to finance or regulate social assistance, he advocated that the state should spend money to protect people from poverty and deprivation. Asserting that peasant and proletarian families alike had a right to a hearth and a home, he called for authorities to build more public housing. He wanted the archaic system of poor relief to be replaced by a welfare state based on a broad range of social legislation directed at breadwinners. And keeping within the tradition of much of French pronatalism, he demanded that parents be given special favours and benefits in return for their service to the nation. Le Play espoused the idea that fatherhood be elevated to the status of a 'fourth estate' comprising France's most select and deserving citizens.

Le Play's influence on pronatalism could be felt in the numerous proposals put before parliament in the last three decades of the nineteenth century. These included bills which prefigured measures that fascists in interwar Italy also considered, such as depriving celibates and childless couples of the right to bequeath property to persons other than the state and empowering the state to appropriate up to two-thirds of the property of people with fewer than three children (Spengler 1938: 232). The National Assembly also debated plans to allow Catholic priests to marry and to withhold voting rights from men aged between 26 and 40 until they had contracted marriage. As well as a celibacy tax, disciples of Le Play pursued fiscal reforms which would, if implemented, have mainly affected the propertied classes. Much of the pronatalist legislative programme during these years favoured middling farmers, family businessmen and small shopkeepers more than it did waged labourers. Two of the financial privileges for families which were repeatedly advocated but not adopted comprised *liberté testamentaire* (testamentary liberty) prohibiting the fragmentation of farms and the non-seizability of the assets, including animals and implements, of indebted farmers (Talmy, vol. 1, 1962: 49).

Exemptions from taxation on income, savings and property for parents with large families figured as a major item on the pronatalist platform. Taxes, like military service, were an obligation to the state which was shared equally by all. But Le Play and his followers were opposed to the democratic principle of equality before the law (Tomlinson 1983: 18). They saw society as an aggregate of individual *pères de famille* who deserved special citizen rights. A reform of 1889 exempted the heads of families of seven or more children from property taxes, but this enactment was abandoned a year later because of its cost to the Treasury. A 1901 law reducing succession duties was an early victory for the pronatalist cause. But advocates of family rights wanted the state to introduce a system of taxation based on transfer payments from the least deserving to the most worthy. They advocated that government should penalize small *familles malthusiennes* with heavy contributions and favour *familles nombreuses* with a full range of exemptions (Talmy, vol. 1, 1962: 74–5).

A new family politics based on the notion of paternal rights emerged in the last decades of the nineteenth century. Though reformist, the programme of Le Play and his disciples constituted a conservative backlash against change. Pronatalist proposals protecting the economic interests of small cultivators, for example, were a defensive reaction against the threats to a rural way of life which industrialization posed. International competition, falling prices and agricultural crisis provoked French farmers to articulate their collective concerns through a pronatalist agenda. French pronatalism was also motivated by preoccupations with social stability. Modern society, Le Play believed, was a seedbed of revolution which had to be reorganized along hierarchical and patriarchal lines if the family and social peace were to be preserved. The memory of the June days in 1848 and the Paris Commune of 1871 kept bourgeois fears of Jacobin revolt alive. French anarchism, syndicalism and socialism promised perpetual class struggles through the weapons of political terrorism, union organization, collective action and the general strike. Economic development and the world depression after 1873 witnessed the rapid growth of the labour movement and worker militancy even among the formerly placid peasantry. These all roused a din of calls for an alternative politics capable of uniting a nation torn by conflict and strife. Pronatalism reflected these widespread anxieties about the social problems engendered by the rise of modern mass society. Prompted by hopes of a new era of class harmony and cooperation, Le Play and his followers astutely realized that the ideology of the family could be used as an instrument of counter-revolution.

Catholics played an important part in putting the family on the political agenda. In 1880, Pope Leo XIII issued a major encyclical, *Arcanum Divinae Sapientiae*, which reaffirmed the sacramental nature and procreative purpose of marriage. Catholicism espoused an idea of marriage as the moral foundation of society which was compatible with the conservative thinking behind much of the pronatalism inspired by Le Play (Prost 1989: 147–50). The Catholic

Church also sought to break the monopoly of the organized Left over the championing of economic issues relating to family welfare. Promulgated in March 1891, Leo XIII's *De Rerum Novarum* was a monumental statement on the 'Condition of the Working Classes' which provoked public debate about social questions. Condemning poverty under industrial capitalism, the encyclical asserted that workers had a right to a just and decent wage sufficient for family survival.

The doctrine of a 'family wage' embodied in the Pope's message spawned a great deal of enthusiasm in France for new legislation to guarantee social justice for all. An accident insurance act of 1898 sought to regulate mutual aid societies and affirm employer responsibility for injuries at work. But this law gave only minimal protection to the work force. Although he was a Catholic priest, Jules Lemire sat in the Chamber as a deputy from the Nord region from 1898 to 1928. Influenced equally by Le Play and by *De Rerum Novarum*, Lemire became a staunch supporter of welfare reform. In 1900, he presented a bill outlining a system of compulsory old-age and sickness insurance based on contributions from the state, employers and workers. However, parliament did not legislate for the aged and infirm until 1905 (Talmy 1962: vol. 1, 49–50). The Vatican's command to the faithful to draw converts to the cause also inspired Catholics to challenge the dominance of the socialist party and the trade union movement of the *Confédération générale du travail* (General Confederation of Labour) by politicizing their pastoral mission and mobilizing support among the proletariat. Although they were a minority group in republican and anticlerical France, Catholics interpreted the Pope's encyclical to mean that they should struggle to become a political force of consequence (Rollet 1955: 40–3).

Political Catholicism tried to turn the ideological orientation of the proletariat away from revolutionary fervour. Organized into a consortium (*L'Association catholique des patrons du Nord*), mill-owners in the textile regions of the North sought to cement relations between capital and labour by christianizing capitalism and creating a corporate order. The charter of the Catholic employers' association asserted that 'the worker is not a force that one utilizes or rejects according only to the needs of production. He is our brother in Jesus Christ, given by God to *patrons* who remain obligated to place him in the proper conditions to facilitate his eternal life'. Patricia Hilden has contended that employer reactions to *De Rerum Novarum* amounted to 'little more than window-dressing' (Hilden 1986:

84–5). But this interpretation underplays the fact that *patrons* who owned family businesses used workplace worship, company welfare schemes, employer patronage of good works and their own brand of Christian paternalism to deflect the political loyalties of the masses away from socialism.

One of the legendary figures of social Catholicism, Léon Harmel (1829–1915) owned a mill in the Val des Bois in the Champagne region where he built a company village and school, as well as a church in which he worshipped every Sunday alongside his workers. Attempting to create a familial atmosphere within the firm, he encouraged his workers to call him *bon père*. Influenced by Le Play, he believed that *patrons* had a moral responsibility to care for the spiritual and material needs of their workers and that workers owed their employers loyalty and obedience. Opposed to the spread of socialist unions, he tried to convince fellow millowners to show benevolence by recognizing Catholic syndicates and introducing collective bargaining to settle disputes. The average pay of a factory worker, Harmel realized, was too low to allow a *chef de famille* to maintain a decent standard of living. He thought that need should determine the size of income of a family and that employers should guarantee at least a minimum subsistence to married men with dependents. In response to *De Rerum Novarum*, Harmel became a chief proponent of the *supplément familial de salaire*, a wage supplement given to workers with families (Rollet 1955: 130–36). He advocated that *patrons* put aside a portion of their profits in a fund to finance these bonuses.

Although often cited by historians as the originator of France's family allowance system, Harmel dispensed wage increments to offset price rises. The amount of his family supplement represented the difference between the estimated cost-of-living and the actual salary. While these supplements were meant to keep in line with inflation and could be withdrawn during a recession, labour had some say in determining their size since they were subject to negotiation with management. Following Harmel's lead, other *patrons* granted *allocations familiales*, family allowances proper. The movement towards family allowances was strongest among owners of the vast textile factories of northern towns like Lille, Roubaix and Tourcoing, and of the huge metallurgical plants of the centre. While Catholic industrialists claimed that they were putting their religious principles into practice by introducing allowances, the system did have certain advantages over other forms of remuneration.

What distinguished a family allowance from a cost-of-living bonus was that *allocations familiales* were a supplement whose size was proportional not to the price index but rather to the number of children under the school-leaving age of 13 that a worker had to support. Because a flat-rate for each dependant was added to the wage-packet, this sum was fixed by employers, and only married workers were entitled to the benefit; family allowances on average added less to the firm's wage bill than did cost-of-living bonuses or pay rises for all workers. Not surprisingly, the *patrons* of thirty or more firms throughout the nation's industrial heartland voluntarily introduced such schemes in the years between 1891 and 1914 alone. Many public authorities in various departments also began to give them to their employees. A few categories of civil servants in the Treasury, Post and Telegraph Office and the Colonial Office were offered child allowances by central government before the war, as were some railwaymen, schoolteachers and officers in the Army and Navy (Vibart 1926: ch. 4; Glass 1967: ch. 3). But before the interwar period, great disparity in the scale of payments existed even among factories in the same sector, employers were not bound to provide them by statutory requirements, and many categories of workers had yet to gain entitlement.

Industrialists defended *allocations* by claiming that they were a *sursalaire*, a supplementary benefit and a 'pure liberality' generously given by *patrons* with a moral conscience and a commitment to social justice. Since they were legally bound to pay only a bare minimum wage, Christian capitalists could somewhat justifiably argue that they acted out of the goodness of their hearts. They were motivated to introduce family allowances, they stated, by recognition that a family man had greater need and responsibility than a single man. But significantly, employers did not want their workers to see allowances as an integral part of wages which was due to them by right. Understandably, some trade unionists contended that *allocations* were a camouflage for wage restraint. By introducing allowances, they argued, employers abolished the principle of equal pay for equal work, stratified the working class, created unfair income inequalities and kept overall labour costs down. Instead of preferential terms of employment for some, they demanded better wage rates and regular cost-of-living bonuses for all, regardless of whether a worker had dependents. Opposition to allowances was based on the belief that *patrons* should provide a standard 'man's wage' which was responsive to inflationary pressures and large enough to maintain an 'average' family of a wife and three children.

Because allowances were supposed to be independent of wages, some labour leaders also objected to any qualifications being placed on entitlement to them. Not payable to strikers or absentees, to those on disability or old-age pensions or, in most cases, to the unemployed, they were calculated on the basis of the number of hours worked weekly, as well as the size of a recipient's family. Workers whose families subsisted on a single income were offered an *allocation de salaire unique*. As this higher rate was granted to the worker whose wife stayed at home, allowances suppressed women's employment and protected the male labour market. In the textile factories which paid allowances to female workers, women received a much smaller sum than their male counterparts received, including those who did the same kind of job. While many French families relied on a mother's earnings to bring them above mere subsistence, *allocations* perpetuated the myths that a woman's place was in the home and that men were the sole breadwinners. Few commentators ever remarked on the fact that families would be far better off, with or without child benefit, if women only enjoyed full equality of opportunity and pay. Given only to workers within an individual company or consortium, allowances also tended to reduce labour turnover and mobility (Vibart 1926: ch. 5; Talmy, vol. 2, 1962: 120–36). Not only were they designed to halt migration to cities, but they were also conceived as a means to create a stable and loyal workforce dependent on employer paternalism.

In spite of disputes over the aims and impact of allowances, the system spread sporadically throughout large firms in private industry in the prewar period. Until 1932, however, employers successfully resisted attempts at state regulation. Catholic *patrons* knew that if allowances were to become statutory, they would lose their appearance of being a gift from a benevolent employer. Christian capitalists saw family allowances as an effective way of deterring the development of class-consciousness among the proletariat. The creation of a stratum of privileged workers fragmented the labour force. Solidarity among workers was more difficult to achieve since they were internally divided by a hierarchy of status and wages. Preferential treatment towards *chefs de famille* also diluted the politics of class struggle in the workplace by encouraging fathers to focus on protecting their own economic self-interest rather than defending collective concerns.

Allowances, then, were not originally conceived by Catholic employers as a pronatalist measure. By inhibiting male migration, however, they may have had a demographic impact upon the communities where rural industry thrived. Undoubtedly, France's relatively low birthrate was one factor behind the rise of the allowance system in the first place, as *patrons* had to attract workers to their employ. An interesting comparison can be made with Italian employers who faced no such compulsion to extend worker welfare schemes. In Italy, chronic over-population created a saturated labour market which perpetuated a low-waged economy. By contrast, prolonged fertility decline, compounded by successive waves of rural flight, gave French workers a bargaining power which their Italian comrades simply did not enjoy.

Renewed anxiety over demographic decline accompanied the spread of family allowances. The year 1896 saw the publication of an official census which confirmed that in four of the previous six years the annual deathrate had exceeded the birthrate. The onset of negative growth deepened the disquiet over France's withering and aged population and coincided with the foundation that year of a neo-Malthusian society, the *Ligue de la régénération humaine* (McLaren 1983). The launch of an intensive birth control campaign by Paul Robin's radical movement further alarmed the *repopulateurs* who appealed for reforms aimed at protecting the French family. Wide recognition that other European powers, and especially the old enemy, a unified and expansionist Germany, still enjoyed buoyant birthrates only worsened the unease. Concerned politicians, prominent intellectuals and private citizens decided to organize a national movement singularly devoted to pressuring government for a pronatalist family policy. At its foundation in May 1896, the National Alliance for the Increase of the French Population (*Alliance nationale pour l'accroissement de la population française*) comprised 116 members, including the writer, Emile Zola, who in 1899 published the pronatalist novel, *Fecundity*, the first of a four-book series on the theme of national regeneration through population growth (Schneider 1990: 41). Taking as its motto the slogan '*le devoir patriotique de la procréation*' (the patriotic duty of procreation), the National Alliance immediately adopted the tactic of active political lobbying among parliament and the public (Talmy, vol. 1, 1962: ch. 2).

The National Alliance soon attracted the widespread publicity and financial backing needed to lobby effectively. Immediately after its formation, the organization launched the first of many vociferous campaigns to alert the nation to the dangers of depopulation. The national leadership, including the deputy, André Honorrat, and the physiologist, Charles Richet, sent over 10,000 copies of its founding manifesto to politicians and administrators at all levels of government and to influential élites, whom it reached through local Chambers of Commerce, men's clubs and employer associations. Patronage from important people was the key to its success, so leaders spared no expense in courting the support of such prominent figures as Edouard Michelin, patriarch of a family of wealthy industrialists (McLaren 1983: 177; Tomlinson 1983: 34–42). By publishing a magazine about infant care targeted at the middle-class housewife, delivering propaganda leaflets door-to-door and eventually distributing a documentary film free-of-charge to cinemas nation-wide, the alliance tried to reach a mass audience (Talmy, vol. 1, 1962: 43; vol. 2: 83–5). The sophisticated style of this strategy to shape public opinion was matched by dedication to the single objective of getting new laws favouring large families on the books. Declaring themselves to be entirely apolitical, members of the alliance bombarded parliamentarians of all persuasions with a vast succession of legislative demands.

The official programme of the alliance announced the creation of a society for propaganda and action devoted to achieving social justice for families. One of the founding members of the movement, Jacques Bertillon repeatedly argued that the financial burdens of childrearing put parents off the idea of large families. Influenced by Le Play, he argued that *chefs de famille* were treated unjustly, and that they should have the right to redemptions from taxation for their dependents (Talmy, vol. 1, 1962: 106). Evaluations for property taxes worked to the detriment of families of three or more children who, he claimed, were penalized with higher rates because they had to occupy big houses. A law of 17 July 1889 granted exemptions to families of seven or more children, but this enactment gave no relief whatsoever to smaller households. Central government had to intervene by ending legal favouritism of any type towards those *familles malthusiennes* who selfishly practised birth control at the expense of the nation's most deserving. Bertillon believed that the 'normal' French family comprising at least three children should receive some form of supplementary assistance from the state and that the 'ideal' family of four or more should be singled out with substantial rewards for their patriotic service to the nation (Tomlinson 1983: ch. 1).

Clearly, Le Play's focus on fiscal reforms continued under the banner of the alliance. The aim of Bertillon's organization was to enshrine the principle of preferential treatment for *familles nombreuses* in existing tax law and then to broaden continually the base of benefits until a whole system of family-based welfare was in place. The alliance wished in the first instance to abolish death duties and to introduce exemptions from direct taxes for families with more than three children. One of their early achievements was to gain recognition from government that the falling birthrate was a political issue of paramount importance to the nation. In July 1900, as many as 131 senators endorsed a resolution calling for the creation of an extra-parliamentary committee on depopulation (Talmy, vol. 1, 1962: 99–105; Tomlinson 1983: 44–5).

Once it was finally established seventeen months later, the commission began work in January 1902 and issued a report in July 1902 which affirmed that the 'development, prosperity and grandeur of France' depended on whether couples of all classes could be encouraged to increase the size of their families by means of financial incentives (Beale 1911: 171–267). Long recognized by the medical profession to be the primary cause of fertility decline, the widespread practice of family planning was also singled out by commissioners as a matter of grave public concern. In particular, the apparently rising rate of abortion and the increasing frequency of its use by married women as a back-up method of birth control was perceived to be a national peril (McLaren 1976: 475–92). The government of Prime Minister René Waldeck-Rousseau which endorsed the commission was particularly alarmed about the military consequences of fertility control. Asserting that France would rank sixth among the great powers and have a population of about half that of Germany should the birthrate continue to decline, pronatalists and politicians alike linked the issue of demographic decline with such pressing concerns as defence planning (Hunter 1962: 490–503). When the extra-parliamentary commission convened in 1911 for the last time, members focused on devising strategies to combat the evils of 'Malthusianism'. Estimating that as many as 500,000 illegal abortions were performed each year, commissioners recommended, unsuccessfully, that the legislature put harsher penalties for these offences on the books. Other measures which were proposed by the commission included a celibacy tax and a tax on childless couples, both of which were eventually introduced.

Historians are quick to point out that no specific legislation emerged either from the 1902 commission on depopulation, which deliberated for almost ten years, or from a second commission which was formed in 1912 and was equally as ineffectual (Tomlinson 1985: 407; Schneider 1990: 42). Although the impact of pronatalism was still rather limited, advocates of a population policy had managed to create a political climate favourable to the cause. In

1911, a pronatalist bloc emerged within parliament and this cross-party alliance attracted the support of senators and deputies. As many as 109 deputies out of 597 immediately became members. One of the leaders of the *Groupe parlementaire pour la protection de la natalité*, Adolphe Landry, a radical deputy and committed pronatalist, helped shape French family policy. As Minister of Labour, Landry presided over the introduction of the new Family Allowance Act of 1932. He published an important pronatalist book, *La révolution démographique* in 1934 and he helped draft the *Code de la famille* in 1939. Ferdinand Buisson, a radical-socialist, acted as the group's first president and Edmond Lefebre du Prey, a prominent conservative, served as its vice-president. According to Richard Tomlinson, only right-wing extremists and far-left socialists (with one exception) were not represented in this broad alliance whose purpose was to promote the passage of pronatalist and familist legislation. The Parliamentary Group for the Protection of Natality increasingly attracted adherents. By the 1914 election, which saw a landslide victory for the Left, 264 out of 502 deputies within the Chamber were avid pronatalists; and by the 1924 election, when the Left won 328 of the 582 seats in parliament, three out of five deputies were committed to the idea of demographic increment (Tomlinson 1983: 56 and 91–7; Talmy, vol. 1, 1962: 158).

As elsewhere in Europe, the war proved to be a major watershed in attitudes towards population. Gustave Hervé, for example, was a leading socialist and advocate of birth control before 1914. But during the hostilities, he experienced an ideological conversion resulting in an outpouring of suppressed nationalist ardour. Longing for a glorious national victory culminating in proletarian revolution, he became a patriot and a pronatalist. The working class, he believed, had to be numerically strong enough to win both the war and the class struggle (Winter 1988: 122–46). Not only was pronatalist nationalism winning over even staunch socialists to the cause of birthrate increase, but it also gained the strong support of French eugenicists. On the whole, French eugenics steered clear of any association with neo-Malthusianism and preferred instead to join forces with the pronatalist movement. In their unwavering commitment to pronatalism and full endorsement of 'positive' social reforms, French eugenicists shared far more in common with their like-minded colleagues in Italy than they did with those in Britain, Germany or America. Partly because of the overwhelming influence of biomedical expertise and hereditarian belief in these countries, eugenics in Britain, Germany and America tended to favour 'negative' measures aimed at preventing 'disgenic' (unhealthy or injurious) individuals from procreating.

British, German and American eugenicists believed that most diseases and defects were inheritable, so the best way to safeguard the race was to prohibit people with any impairments from passing these on to future generations. They also argued that favourable variations acquired by one generation could not be transmitted to the next. No amount of environmental influence could alter the fact that 'inferior' qualities were preserved, either in a latent or dominant state, through the course of evolution. For common cultural reasons, however, French and Italian eugenicists proved to be receptive to environmentalist arguments that improvements in health, education and welfare could produce beneficial modifications in the innate qualities of individuals which were inheritable. Changes in social conditions, they maintained, could modify nature. They also came to the conclusion that since many sicknesses, such as epilepsy and haemophilia, were probably caused by recessive genes anyway, there was no point in trying to eradicate these by the imprecise method of birth control.

French eugenics allied with French pronatalism. The leader of the National Alliance, Jacques Bertillon, participated in the First International Eugenics Conference in July 1912 and coordinated the participation of the large French delegation. Charles Richet, one of the co-founders of Bertillon's pronatalist organization, also served as vice-president of the French Eugenics Society which was founded in December 1912. Leading eugenicists in France had contributed their expertise to the deliberations of the 1902 Senate Commission on Depopulation (Schneider 1982: 274; 1990: 84–91). French eugenics also cultivated close contacts with Italian eugenics. British, German and American scientists and doctors cooperated actively among themselves and led a radical wing within the international eugenics federation which adhered to a 'negative' selectionist programme. French and Italian eugenicists, on the other hand, moved cosily into a partnership based on their advocacy of a more moderate environmentalist platform. In 1935, this alliance led to the foundation of a separate international eugenics federation of 'Latin' countries under the leadership of Corrado Gini, president of the newly-named Italian Society of Genetics and Eugenics. At the inaugural meeting of 'Latin' eugenicists in Mexico City, delegates from Italy and France were joined by those from Romania, Belgium, Mexico, Peru, Catalonia, Brazil and twelve other Latin American nations. Eugenics in these Catholic and 'Latin' countries was decidedly softer than those varieties which developed in Protestant, 'Nordic' and 'Anglo-Saxon' countries (Leys Stepan 1990: 111; Quine forthcoming pt. 1).

During the First World War, French eugenicists, like their colleagues in other countries, became increasingly concerned with the quality of the population. The doctors who comprised a majority of the society's membership worried that the war would have a 'dysgenic' effect on public health. The prevalence of such social ills as illegitimacy and prostitution seemed to have increased as a consequence of wartime mobilization, while the incidence of such biological threats to the race as syphilis and infant mortality seemed to have risen (March 1921: 243–65). Despite recognition that there was probably a significant proportion of the population who were unhealthy as a result of the war, however, French eugenicists shied away from endorsing any 'negative' proposals beyond mass medical screening and premarital testing for disease. For much of the decade following the cessation of hostilities, the movement devoted itself to a campaign for 'positive' remedies for racial degeneration, thereby avoiding any ideological confrontation with the pronatalists.

None the less, despite the extent of pronatalist sentiment in France, one of the problems faced by reformists of all kinds was the reality that the Third Republic's system of unstable coalition government was an obstacle to the development of long-term policies of any kind. A long succession of different administrations would introduce, then withdraw legislation. From one budget to the next, important laws were amended or scrapped. A pronatalist consensus of sorts was indeed beginning to emerge even before 1914, though this would only slowly begin to have an impact. Family policy in France developed unevenly through piecemeal legislation. Fiscal conservatism further precluded the passage of a body of laws which would have required substantial increases in taxation and public spending. Another hindrance to the emergence of a full population programme, disagreement still prevailed about the best way to alter fertility. The prevalence of pronatalist sentiment within politics and society did not preclude real differences of approach to the problem of depopulation. Some populationists believed in the power of welfare reform directed at mothers and children to reduce levels of mortality, while others advocated measures favouring only large families. Pronatalist politicians also failed to achieve any unanimity of opinion about whether quality or quantity, or a mixture of both, should be encouraged. Despite these divisions, there was a growing broad base of support for the idea of population increase.

A distinct politics about family and population issues arose in the early years of the Third Republic. Due to the presence of the pro-alliance lobby in the nation's capital, Paris was undoubtedly the epicentre of pronatalist civic activism in France. But by the first decades of the century, a so-called 'family movement' had gained momentum in the provinces as well. Never more than a patchwork of associations of concerned citizens, this movement is an intriguing illustration of the formidable potential for the mobilization of a plurality of special interests around family issues. The growing sectionalism of political life in the prewar period was reflected in the rise of diverse pressure groups lobbying government for legislation to protect their own particularist interests. Much more needs to be known about the membership, propaganda and activities of family associations before a coherent picture can emerge, but some observations may be made. French fathers throughout the nation were beginning to see themselves as a disadvantaged group who had to organize locally in order to increase their influence over national policy. The social groups that fall within the broad category of the middle class began to form these family associations. Independent property owners, such as farmers, shopkeepers, artisans and businessmen, allied with members of the liberal professions and salaried employees, such as teachers and civil servants, to press for a political voice. The politics of the family in France served as a pretext for the assertion of the class interests of the *bourgeoisie*.

The first of many such organizations to emerge, the *Famille Montpelliéraine* was founded in 1894 by the mayor and the élite of Montpellier. Like many others of its kind, this league drew its support from local notables, professionals and philanthropists. An expression of clerical and charitable concerns in the community, the Montpellian family functioned as a Catholic mutual aid society administering sickness and maternity compensation plans for members. Sponsored fund-raising events and membership dues also helped to subsidize the running of a cooperative store and a housewifery school where women were trained in domestic management. In Montpellier, the ideological trappings of familism served to bolster the collective strength and confidence of a lay Catholic establishment devoted to extending the provision of aid for families. The group's self-help schemes also filled a gap in a system of departmental and municipal welfare which remained scant throughout the prewar period (Tomlinson 1985: 405). An association of Fecund Fathers was formed in 1908 in the department of the Saône-et-Loire whose aim was to honour particularly prolific men with financial support and public praise. The society distributed cash subsidies to fathers who had at least seven children. Its existence reflected the widespread belief that *chefs de famille* were a special category of loyal citizens whose reproductive service to the nation should be valued and emulated by all (Talmy, vol. 1, 1962: 140).

Other associations functioned as political pressure groups lobbying for concessions from government for *familles nombreuses*. Created in 1907, the Departmental Alliance of Fathers of Large Families derived patronage from the propertied and professional middle classes. Leaders of the Departmental Alliance wished to attract a large following and to create a nation-wide network of support for a population programme based on favouritism towards *chefs de famille*. Lay Catholics organized themselves into their own parent leagues devoted to moral reform. By 1908, fifty such groups already existed in confessional strongholds across the country and the main areas of concern of these groups were education and the curriculum. Activists defended their right to send their children to segregated Church schools where they would be safe from the pernicious influences of the anticlerical Republic. Showing a great deal of organizational acumen, committed Catholics drew on their long-established communal traditions to build a wide institutional apparatus for civic activism. Consolidated into a national league in 1912, *L'Union des associations catholiques de chefs de famille* (The Union of Catholic Associations of Heads of Families) comprised twenty-two regional federations representing 659 affiliated associations by 1914 (Talmy, vol. 1, 1962: 152).

One of the more eccentric movements to emerge in the prewar period was the Paris-based *Ligue populaire des pères et mères de familles nombreuses* (Popular League of Fathers and Mothers of Big Families), which was founded by Captain Simon Maire in 1908. A father of either ten or twelve children (depending on the source), Maire was an ex-military man and practising Catholic who managed to create a truly popular family movement. Open to any parent of at least four children, the association was one of the few which offered free membership in an attempt to attract broad allegiance. By 1911, his movement had 600,000 members (including men, women and children), a figure which compared favourably to the 3,455 who supported the National Alliance for the Protection of the French Population (Tomlinson 1983: 105). Deeply influenced by social Catholics like La Tour du Pin, Maire wished to bring into being a new Christian corporate order which privileged the family and traditional values. Deep religious convictions were not his sole motivating force, though, for his military training provided the inspiration behind the league's unique organization and tactics. Believing that the time had come for 'direct action not words', Maire maintained that protest rather than propaganda would push government into action. He envisaged his movement as a militant, mass army of clerical combatants committed to a policy of non-violent political disruption. Members were organized into local sections which engaged in disciplined suffragette-style disturbances to focus public attention on the cause. Although it was not anti-republican, his organization sought to break the political immobilism which characterized coalition government in the Third Republic.

Much to the dismay of the establishment, Maire's campaigners behaved more like Christian storm-troopers than respectable family men and women. A crowd of league supporters held a huge demonstration in Paris in April 1911 which municipal authorities tried to stop by sending in the police. In the chaos that followed, a number of arrests were made, including that of Maire, who declared himself to be a martyr to the cause. Maire won a great publicity coup when city officials moved quickly to denounce the prefect of police for allowing his men to use undue force. Because of the adverse press coverage which the incident attracted, President Raymond Poincaré intervened personally the following year by inviting the organization to hold a mass pronatalist *songfest* along the Quay d'Orsay and by sending along government representatives (Rollet 1955: 100). Although he had no children of his own, Poincaré was an ardent pronatalist.

As a reflection of a growing mobilization of pronatalist nationalism among parliament and the public, the government began to lay the basis for a systematic population policy. Substantive social welfare laws were enacted which gradually extended the rights of citizens, in principle if not always in practice. An enactment in 1904 obligated each department to create a maternity home (*maison maternelle*) staffed by doctors who were qualified to give needy women prenatal care and advice. Like an earlier act in 1893 which entitled poor pregnant women to free medical assistance, this reform aimed at preventing abortion, infanticide and child abandonment, as well as reducing prenatal and neonatal mortality. Completely discretionary in character, however, this legislation did not prevent departmental and municipal governments from evading their responsibility to provide medical services for the nation's mothers (Talmy, vol. 1, 1962: 107–10).

The government was also motivated by concern for the health of babies born to working mothers and to those who were alone and destitute. A law of June 1913 awarded pregnant women with no other means of support a somewhat meagre monthly subsidy during the last month of pregnancy and the first two months after delivery. The legislation also stipulated that working women were entitled to maternity benefit amounting to a portion of their normal salary or wages. Restrictive conditions limited the impact of this law. A mere pittance when the loss of earnings from waged work is considered, this benefit was given only to those who agreed to stay at home for the whole of an eight-week period of leave. In addition to these entitlements, women without any financial resources could receive a family allowance for the maintenance of their children for as long as two years after the birth of each child. Although ambitious in scope, overriding budget constraints somewhat diminished the effects of this reform. Remaining in force until 1939, the enactment was finally amended by the *Code de la famille*, which promised to bring the rate of maternity benefit in line with inflation (Tomlinson 1983: 99).

Another indication that parliament was prepared to enact familist legislation came in July 1913 when a significant reform was passed which took effect in January 1914. This new family allowance act established the principle in welfare law that poverty was linked to family size. Large families were now deemed to be a special category of the poor who deserved additional means-tested assistance because of the disproportionate drain childcare costs placed on limited household budgets. The law granted subsistence aid in the form of an allowance which was paid to fathers or, in the absence of the male head of household, to lone mothers who had at least three children. The benefit was paid out for each child the parent had who was between the ages of 3 and 13 years. If the parent was a widow, she was entitled to a benefit for every child after her first; and if the parent was a widower, he was entitled to an allowance for every child after his second. The assumption behind his peculiar differential was that women were more prone to poverty than men. A parent could claim as much as 90 francs per child per year, a fairly sizeable amount in 1913 but one whose real value decreased with time (Tomlinson 1983: 100–1). By the postwar period, pronatalists argued that the allowance was equal in value to about 75 kilogrammes of bread a year, hardly enough to ensure a decent standard of living to a poor family.

Critics charged that the *allocations* never amounted to much of an income support since the rates failed to keep pace with inflation.

Departments and communes shared the cost of this package, while central government did not contribute any more than its usual grant to local authorities. During periods of economic downturn when resources shrank, the interest of government lay in cutting social spending. After a period of wartime price rices, the fixed maximum rate rose to 200 francs in 1919. In July 1922, an amendment was ratified which temporarily reduced the allowance to 90 francs, but entitled unmarried men and women to the benefit for the first time. After 1923, the rate of aid to families increased steadily but not substantially. During the years of depression and austerity from 1929 to 1936, when France had eighteen different administrations, the level of provision was once again slashed by finance ministers who could not balance the budget. Not all indigent families even qualified for a child maintenance benefit, since only the registered poor could apply. This restrictive condition effectively disqualified those who were working but low-waged from this means-tested form of welfare. With a maximum ceiling set on the amount of aid given, allowances failed to satisfy those who wanted the state to provide a system of supplementary benefits which gave families a decent standard of living. Another limitation of the legislation, assistance, apart from the exceptions noted earlier, was only provided for the fourth and each additional child, thereby excluding many smaller but no less needy families from aid (Tomlinson 1983: 144 and 199; 1985: 407; Reynolds 1990: 173–97; Offen 1991: 141).

The year 1914 also brought significant changes to tax law. In July, income tax contributions were graduated according to family size. Reductions in property taxes for dependents, including wives, came into effect in July 1917. A male head-of-household was now entitled to claim concessions of as much as 7.5 per cent for his first two dependants and 15 per cent for each other dependant. A Centre–Right coalition, the *bloc national*, obtained victory in the election of November 1919. While they were canvassing voters, candidates from both the Left and the Right are reputed to have added the title of '*Père de la famille*' after their other qualifications and to have listed the number of their children in their campaign leaflets and posters (Talmy, vol. 2, 1962: 30–2).

Under the premiership of Alexandre Millerand, the new govern-ment and its ministry contained many self-professed pronatalists, such as J. L. Breton, a republican socialist with five children who became the new Finance Minister. Millerand endorsed the creation of a *Conseil supérieur de natalité* committed to developing pronatal-ist legislation. And he presided over the introduction of a law against 'antinatalist propaganda' which was passed by the Chamber of Deputies with a massive majority of 521 votes to 55. Whoever was found guilty of propagating information about birth control now faced a punishment of six months' imprisonment and a hefty fine; and abortionists were now liable to a maximum sentence of three years (Talmy, vol. 2, 1962: 11). Millerand's government set a precedent which successive administrations followed. Laws against abortion became increasingly harsh until 1942, when legislation introduced by the Vichy regime made it a crime against the state, the race and the nation which was punishable by death. In May 1920, the Third Republic marked Mothers' Day with public celebrations throughout the nation in which about 30,000 mothers of five or more children were awarded medals of honour for their patriotic service to the nation (Offen 1991: 138). While Breton had wanted the government to establish a system of birth premiums entitling particularly prolific women to large, one-off cash payments, the Superior Council for Natality chose instead to lavish praise on these exemplary citizens by giving them bronze, silver and gold medallions.

On 25 July 1920, the legislature introduced an innovation to the system of taxation which was punitive in nature. For the first time, both male and female celibates over 30 years of age were required to pay a 25 per cent surcharge on their income tax payments, while childless couples who had been married for at least ten years saw their contributions increase by 10 per cent (Talmy, vol. 1, 1962: 163–5). That same year, big rail companies began to offer large families savings on return fares for long-distance travel for the whole family. By 1921, a new law entitled *familles nombreuses* to a family railcard which gave them unlimited reductions on train and museum tickets. By the 1920s, *chefs de famille* enjoyed a range of sizeable deductions from taxation, as well as other financial concessions. In 1922, the government introduced legislation which granted them preferential treatment in eligibility for rented accommodation in public housing estates Fathers with many children could now jump the queue in long waiting lists for affordable flats. But pronatalist legislation which cost the Treasury money was vulnerable to economic fluctuations. In 1934, the government implemented financial decrees which, according to one historian, 'virtually abolished', if only temporarily, the tax breaks that fathers of large families had enjoyed since before the war (Tomlinson 1983: 199).

The legislative reforms which successive governments introduced did not amount to much of a true *politique de la famille* (family policy), a fact which did not escape the notice of populationists.

Family associations continued to proliferate, due in no small measure to public awareness of the demographic consequences of the war. That France suffered far more war dead and wounded than any other belligerent nation in Western Europe undoubtedly sustained the momentum of pronatalism. The social change engendered by wartime mobilization also broadened the family movement further, as new groups with diverse objectives emerged. With illegitimacy, single-parenthood and infant mortality on the rise during the war, many more people became concerned with the question of the quality of the population. Founded in 1916 by a professor at the Catholic Institute in Paris, *Pour la vie* (the Pro-Life Movement) campaigned actively on behalf of religious and family values. Although they were influenced by Le Play, pro-lifers believed that economic concessions alone would fail to revive the birthrate. According to them, a spiritual cleansing of the nation was needed to rid decadent France of pornography, prostitution, the cinema and birth control. Allying themselves with the League of Public Morality and the National Temperance Society, pro-lifers were as pronatalist as *Alliance Nationale* supporters, but their ideological orientation differed from the secular pronatalism of Bertillon. Advocating that each individual should have at least four children, they believed that procreation was not a political duty so much as a moral obligation. While they were firmly opposed to any 'artificial' means of contraception, and singled out abortion as a particularly heinous crime against the unborn child, they countenanced recourse to so-called 'Christian Malthusianism' by married couples, a term they defined as sexual abstinence and 'natural' birth control. With 8,000 members by 1918, the organization failed to gain much influence among politicians since its overt clericalism found little sympathy in republican circles (Tomlinson 1983: 117; Prost 1989: 147–64).

But the existence of *Pour la vie* demonstrated to what extent familism could become a platform for conservative moralism. Sexuality was a fertile source of moral panic, and especially so since the war seemed to have undermined French motherhood. The belief that many Frenchwomen had been raped by German soldiers compounded unease about prostitution and illegitimacy, as well as a falling birthrate. At the beginning of the war, the Defence, Interior and Finance ministries worked closely with the presidency to evolve strategies for population control. As in other belligerent countries, French wartime domestic policy was motivated by concern that contagious diseases such as typhoid, syphilis and dysentery should be combated effectively by the introduction of measures for social hygiene (March 1921: 243–65). The war also prompted the state to expand welfare provision for mothers and to supervise women's work in munitions industries. In August 1914, Senator Paul Strauss, president of the League Against Infant Mortality, established a Central Office for Maternal and Infant Assistance under governmental patronage (Reynolds 1990: 180). A well-known eugenicist and authority on public health matters, Strauss had also been a member of the 1902 commission on depopulation. His office oversaw the introduction of protective legislation. In 1914, an emergency law granted needy women whose husbands were soldiers a daily family allowance for each child they had under the age of 6 years. The government subsidized the establishment of free nursery schools within working-class neighbourhoods and of crèches at the work place. It also tried to prevent working women from turning to 'artificial' substitutes for breastfeeding. In 1917, a new enactment prohibited the sale of feeding bottles; and in 1918, a decree regulated the manufacture of powdered and condensed milk products for babies (Bernard 1929: 7 and ch. 24).

In the postwar period, feminist groups of all political persuasions unwittingly provoked a male reaction when they intensified pressure on parliament to give women the vote. The women's movement suffered a staggering defeat in 1923 when the Senate decided against permitting female suffrage (Cova 1991: 119–37). Demands for women's emancipation only increased fears that the family was under attack. Perceived to be the consequences of the rise of modern society, birth control, prostitution, divorce, female suffrage and women's work outside the home symbolized to many observers that France was undergoing pronounced moral decline. Reflecting general anxiety about the threat of women's advancement, conservatives like the pro-lifers maintained a vision of the social order in which the family had a policing role. For them, the family regulated sexuality, reinforced a division of sex roles and inculcated respect for authority. The institution of motherhood also helped to solidify society by keeping women in their appropriate place. The tumult caused by war and its aftermath brought pronatalist, familist and maternalist concerns to the forefront of public debate. The issues of family welfare, the protection of motherhood and the birthrate were becoming indistinguishable (Huss 1990: 56).

Founded in 1918, the *Ligue des droits de la famille* (League for the Rights of the Family) refuted the revolutionary principles of 1789 embodied in the Rights of Man. Influenced by Le Play, the conservative and pronatalist organization sought to redefine citizenship and reward *chefs de famille* with special political and social privileges. Like so many other family associations, the league represented the interests of male heads-of-household and permitted women to become members only through their husbands (Talmy, vol. 1, 1962: 198). A clerico-natalist association which shared the belief in the family as a refuge from the moral chaos outside the home, *La plus grande famille* (The Biggest Family) was established by two industrialists, Auguste Isaac and Achille Glorieux. Elitist in aims, the association offered membership only to good Catholics and well-to-do parents with at least five children. Isaac was a wealthy businessman, a father of eleven children and a commerce minister in the cabinet under Millerand. Like Isaac, Achille Glorieux saw himself as a Christian crusader with a mission to promote the development of a *politique familiale* (family policy). Glorieux was also a leader of the Association of Catholic Employers of the North who had encouraged the spread of the family allowance system in the prewar period (Talmy, vol 1, 1962: 253).

Because of the civic activism and religious belief of people like Isaac and Glorieux, pronatalism grew into a mass phenomenon and a significant social force in France. In the early 1920s, the movement comprised nine national associations, including the *Alliance nationale*, sixty-two regional associations and eleven departmental federations of *familles nombreuses*, totalling more than 500 different groups representing more than 95,000 families (Ogden and Huss 1982: 291). At the height of its influence in the years before the Wall Street Crash, the National Alliance for the Protection of the French Birthrate had 40,000 members, a small percentage of the total membership of pronatalist organizations. By 1930, over 300,000 families had joined associations which existed in all but a few departments throughout the republic. The vast majority of pronatalists in France were members of family associations, so clerical pronatalism undoubtedly predominated over the secular variety espoused by the National Alliance. The dominance of a brand of conservative pronatalism which grew out of political Catholicism was further evidenced by the fact that Catholic strongholds had particularly high concentrations of pronatalist groups. In the North, for example, local pronatalist associations of large families numbered as many as 253 in 1921 and they continued to proliferate in the postwar period. Mobilization on this scale was an extraordinary achievement (Talmy, vol. 2, 1962: 53–73 and 247).

Despite ideological differences, the pronatalist movement was moving towards greater unity in order to increase its influence over policy formation. In 1919, Auguste Isaac presided over the first of many annual congresses where delegates from diverse pronatalist and familist associations met to discuss their shared interests. Two years later, Isaac founded the *Fédération nationale des associations de familles nombreuses* (National Federation of Associations for Large Families), an umbrella organization seeking to unify the movement into a powerful political lobby (Prost 1989: 153). Parliamentarians from all major parties, as well as members of the French Academy, were present at the first *Congrès national de la natalité et des familles nombreuses* at Nancy (National Congress for Natality and Large Families), attended by over 700 delegates. Thereafter, conferences were held nationally and locally until 1938. The 1919 conference endorsed a number of resolutions, including one calling for an extension of family allowances. In 1920, another conference was held in Lille, and this one passed a declaration entitled the *Droits de la famille*, an extraordinary document in the form of a bill of rights. Based on very conservative ideas, the Rights of the Family maintained that the family was a sacred and hierarchical institution founded on marriage and paternal authority whose purpose was the perpetuation of human life. In addition to demanding the usual fiscal concessions directly influenced by Le Play, such as testamentary and taxation reforms, the charter also affirmed that the state should help *chefs de famille* provide their families with a decent standard of living. Work, property and a wage sufficient for a family were deemed to be inviolable rights enjoyed by fathers (Talmy, vol. 1, 1962: 236–7).

The Rights of the Family also proposed that fathers be given a 'family vote'. One of the more peculiar elements of French pronatalism, the concept of *suffrage familial* had a long history. At the turn of the century, some radicals endorsed bills for a family vote because they saw it as a way to enfranchise women. Based on the principle that widows be allowed to vote on behalf of their dead husbands, a family vote could be perceived as a first step towards granting all women citizenship rights. The *Droits de la famille*, however, divorced the idea of a family vote from the question of female suffrage. Supporters of the declaration based their demand for a family vote on the claim that a *père de famille* ought to have a right to at least three votes: one for himself, one for his wife, and one for his children.

Advocates of the family vote argued that France had forty million inhabitants, only ten million of whom could vote. Men below the age of 21, as well as women and children, were effectively deprived of representation. 'Celibates' numbered about six million, a significant percentage of the electorate. Many of these were young men without the family responsibilities which brought maturity of judgement to the exercise of citizenship. Members of families with more than three children constituted over half of the total population. A family vote, proponents believed, would stabilize the political order since fathers of families tended to be older and more conservative than single men (Toulemon 1933: 13–18 and 33–6). From 1906, when parliament first discussed a proposal for a family vote, the issue was repeatedly debated and defeated until the mid 1930s. *Suffrage familial* never became a reality, despite the fact that many parliamentarians supported the notion that fathers be made into a special 'estate'. Politicians, historians agree, were afraid that the introduction of family suffrage would give women the vote by default. Men feared that since women were a majority of the population, female suffrage would tip the balance of political power in their favour and undermine a parliamentary system based on male domination (Tomlinson 1983: 157–66).

Despite the failure of pronatalists to influence electoral reform in the 1920s, a significant achievement for the cause came with the introduction of the Family Allowance Act in 1932. Generally considered by scholars to mark the real beginning of family policy in France, the enactment put family allowances under state regulation for the first time. As Glass has rightly remarked, however, the new legislation did not fundamentally change a system which had grown through private initiative. The new law aimed both to extend provision to categories of workers, such as those employed in agriculture, who were still excluded from entitlement and to create uniformity in the various rates being offered by different enterprises. Under the old system, employers channelled a portion of their profits into an account whose interest paid for the cost of the allowances. After 1918, industrialists began to join together to form associations which pooled contributions and put them into *caisses de compensation*. The creation of compensation funds removed the temptation of individual employers to hire only single men because they were less expensive. Gradually, a number of funds started to subsidize not only ordinary family allowances, which were paid monthly over a number of years, but also birth and even nursing premiums. These were lump sums given as encouragements to female workers to stay home during the confinement and to breast-feed their babies for a long period. By 1925, family allowances had spread so widely that an estimated three million waged workers and salaried employees were covered by them. Pronatalists finally grasped the idea that they could be used to stimulate the birthrate. Beginning in 1919, the National Alliance and other organizations began to lobby government to make their introduction compulsory for all employers (Vibart 1926: 32 and ch. 6).

Under the 1932 guidelines, the old system remained substantially unaltered although state involvement increased. The new legislation made allowances compulsory and set minimum rates of payment. But to avoid increasing the wage bills of industrialists too rapidly, family allowances were to be introduced gradually to the whole of the workforce over a number of years. While agricultural workers gained entitlement in 1932, domestic workers remained excluded until 1939. The state did now contribute to regional compensation funds, but these subsidies were small and the financial burden still fell mainly on employers. According to Glass, the impact of family allowances on the household budgets of working families should not be underestimated.

Rough estimates by the government claimed that an *allocation* paid to an unskilled, manual labourer with four children could increase his family's income by between 10 and 15 per cent. If both a mother and father worked, only the male wage-earner received an allowance. Furthermore, allowances were paid directly to the mother only in industries which had a predominance of female workers, such as textiles. The 1932 legislation did not abolish the gender bias of the system which had developed by private initiative. Male workers were still entitled to higher rates of payment, especially when their wives did not work outside the home. And *allocations* were still perceived as a benefit awarded to male heads-of-household. Nor did the 1932 enactment equalize the rates of allowances paid out by private industry and the public sector. Government employees still received substantially higher allowances than did factory workers, both manual and clerical.

Despite these shortcomings, however, the 1932 act did set an important precedent. Family allowances now became fully integrated into a national system of welfare based on the principle of social justice. The compulsory character and the state regulation of allowances transformed the nature of this benefit. Now enshrined in law as a right of the entire working population, family allowances could no longer be used by paternalistic employers as an instrument of social control. Their function as a pronatalist measure was emphasized repeatedly by government officials who seemed to be over-optimistic about the possible effects of financial incentives on fertility levels. In both fascist Italy and republican France, statesmen clung to the hope that economic rewards for procreation would encourage people to have more babies. But there was no available evidence that demographic patterns could be altered by means of positive eugenic inducements.

Since allowances came no way near towards compensating parents for the full cost of childcare, their impact on the birthrate was bound to be limited. While they did supplement earnings and provide a financial support for families, they were not substantial enough to affect the reproductive behaviour of individuals. Failing in their aim to increase the size of the population, allowances did not cause natality to rise during the interwar period. The most that can be said about their influence on fertility is that they may have halted the spread of the two-child family, but they certainly did not convince people to have larger families (Spengler 1938: 254).

But *allocations* did raise the living standards of families, and to this extent they improved the quality of a significant proportion of the population. Somewhere between five and six million industrial workers out of a total factory workforce of nine million received family allowances in 1938. When railway workers, miners and government employees are added, well over seven million people were covered by the scheme. The cost of this provision continually increased as well, even though the rates of payment generally failed to keep pace with inflation. By the end of the Second World War, France redistributed a sizeable percentage of its national income to families in the form of direct economic aid (Glass 1967: ch. 2; Huss 1990: 64). An unskilled labourer with three children earned a family allowance worth half his pay in 1946, while a factory worker with five children received an allowance which actually exceeded his wage (Prost 1989: 155). But the expansion of selective and family-based forms of welfare was, to a certain extent, achieved to the detriment of other types of assistance, especially those based on the collectivist principle of the universal right of all citizens to live above subsistence.

While France devoted a high percentage of its Gross Domestic Product to protect families with at least three children from poverty, the provision of social security and pensions may have suffered somewhat as a result of the pronatalist bias in the legislation. Not until 1946 did parliament legislate to establish a comprehensive and national scheme for sickness, unemployment and old-age insurance. The extent of state largesse towards *familles nombreuses*, however, should not be overestimated. As Spengler quite rightly pointed out, public spending on family allowances and other kinds of procreative incentives amounted to less than one-third of the sum the Treasury shed annually on defence in the years 1936–7 (Spengler 1938: 254). Financed by both private and public contributions, allowances relieved the state of the full burden of funding. And if it is true that they were extended at the expense of wage increases for the entire labour force, then workers themselves bore some of the cost of a system which excluded many of them from entitlement.

Family allowances became the pivot of French population policy primarily because they were a measure which both the Left and the Right could endorse. When the Popular Front came to power in June 1936, a leftist coalition of radical, socialist and communist parties governed under Léon Blum for two years. Although Blum did not define pronatalism as a political objective, he still increased the state contribution to the allowance system and made the public provision of income support for the family a chief government priority. His administration may have downplayed the pronatalist aspects of welfare policy, but it did determine to decrease infant mortality by expanding social assistance for poor parents. Hitler's reoccupation of the Rhineland in March 1936 reawakened old fears of German aggression, but the Popular Front government refused to pander to nationalistic calls for a public campaign to boost the birthrate. When the radical republican, Edouard Daladier, became Premier in April 1938, he put the problem of *dénatalité* (a declining birthrate) once again at the top of the political agenda. Unlike its immediate predecessor, Daladier's premiership was responsive to the demands of the pronatalist lobby. In June 1938, Daladier introduced decrees which he promised would lay the basis for a comprehensive family-based population policy whose goal was demographic increment through social and moral reform. Seven months later, he announced the creation of a *Haut comité de la population*, a team of experts including prominent eugenicists and pronatalists which drafted the Family Code that was eventually promulgated on 29 July 1939 (Tomlinson 1983: 255).

The *Code de la famille* embodied many of the religious and conservative values which had informed French familist and pronatalist ideas since the nineteenth century. As Karen Offen has contended, it 'privileged a prescriptive family model, explicitly depicted in terms of a male breadwinner and stay-at-home wife with three children and a first child born within two years after marriage' (Offen 1991: 150). Repressive anti-abortion clauses satisfied those who felt that previous legislation had not been harsh enough to act as a real deterrent. Under the code's new guidelines, a convicted abortionist now faced up to ten years' imprisonment, while a woman found guilty of having procured an abortion could be jailed for up to two years. The code introduced a one-off cash allowance in the form of a birth premium which was to be given to a couple who had their first child in the first two years of their marriage. It also devoted many passages to measures designed to combat the adverse effects of modern industrial society on the diminishing birthrate.

The Popular Front government, Daladier believed, had accelerated the decline of the French family by expanding welfare which favoured the urban worker who practised birth control over the rural peasant who still reproduced prolifically. The code proposed to 'repopulate' the countryside by means of government subsidies to keep young people from migrating to cities. Under a scheme very much like similar Nazi legislation, newly-wed farmers were entitled to a generous marriage loan to set up household if they agreed to stay in agriculture for at least ten years. The state also promised to contribute to rural compensation funds and extend family allowances to agricultural workers and self-employed artisans at the same rate which factory workers received (Talmy, vol. 2, 1962: 235–40 and Tomlinson 1983: 265–6). Designed to stop rural flight, these measures seemed a fitting culmination to decades of campaigning which began with Le Play. Many pronatalists were pleased that Daladier's government seemed committed to preserving the 'Republic of Peasants'.

The code unified existing family legislation and extended state provision. But the government had no time to implement reforms since war broke out only five months after the code was promulgated. Daladier led France into war against Germany, but he was replaced by Paul Reynaud in March 1940 and subsequently arrested by Vichy officials. In the spring of 1940, German forces invaded northern France and in June they paraded victoriously through a deserted Paris. Reynaud's government retreated to Bordeaux and then handed power over to Marshal Philippe Pétain, an 84-year-old veteran of the First World War. Pétain had long-standing ties with the *Comité d'action française* (Committee for French Action), the militantly right-wing and Catholic movement which was formed in 1898 by Charles Maurras at the height of the Dreyfus affair. Like Maurras, Pétain was deeply anti-republican, anti-parliamentary and reactionary. He believed that he had a duty to restore France to the powerful and prolific nation it had allegedly been before 1789. On 17 June, Pétain made a historic speech to the French people asking them to lay down their weapons and accept defeat by Germany. After the surrender and armistice, France was divided into two: a zone in the North and West, which was occupied by the Germans, and an unoccupied zone in the Centre and South, which became the collaborationist Vichy regime. Granted full powers to consolidate a personal dictatorship, Pétain committed his government to a programme of National Regeneration which advocated a return to traditional French values and institutions. Long considered by the right to be the pillars of French society, the family and the Church figured prominently in the Vichy regime's ideology and policy for a New Moral Order (Paxton 1972: 3–50).

Under the motto 'Work, Family, and Nation', Pétain's government promised to 'deindustrialize' France and make it a peasant country once more. Determined to protect the *patrie*, the government integrated the *Code de la famille* into an aggressively nationalist, pronatalist and familist programme. Historians, however, have emphasized that only the code's more repressive measures against birth control and abortion were actually implemented and extended during the Second World War. The promised expansion of family allowances, and other 'positive' welfare reforms, would have to wait until the Liberation before they became reality. However limited in impact it may have been, Vichy's family politics helped to consolidate a regime whose claim to authority was otherwise rather shaky. Born at a moment of national defeat and division, the Vichy regime was more in need than most governments of a legitimating ideology which served to embody guiding principles and to mobilize popular support.

Populistic appeals to traditional French and family values, followed by institutional changes favouring the mobilization of society by the state, encouraged people to give their allegiance to Vichy. A ruralist 'back to the soil' rhetoric accompanied attempts to resurrect the French family along patriarchal lines. Ruralism added to the power of a universalistic pronatalist ideology which attempted to persuade disempowered citizens that Vichy stood for all that was best in France. Together with the Church, the Army provided an institutional mainstay to a dictatorship devoted to militarizing and disciplining civil society. The creation of the *Chantiers de la jeunesse*, the state-run youth movement, aimed at training children to be loyal citizens and patriots (Griffiths 1970: 257). Pronatalism served as the ideological cement for an authoritarian regime seeking to recruit the young, integrate the masses and politicize private life. The drive against abortion became a national crusade as the Vichy regime searched frantically for causes which bolstered its self-image as the guardian of traditional family values. In February 1942, a new law was passed which made abortion a crime against the state. The National Alliance and factions of the family movement applauded this move by the government to preserve the morality of the people. The campaign of police repression which followed finally culminated in the much-publicized execution in July 1943 of a woman accused of being an abortionist (Tomlinson 1983: 273). Under Vichy, all the various conservative strands within French pronatalism were distilled into an official ideology and policy which openly sacrificed the rights of women to the greater interests of the family and the nation.

Certain conclusions can be drawn about the peculiarities of French pronatalism. The influence of clerical pronatalism predominated in French population policy despite the existence of a secular brand advocated by the National Alliance. By the end of the 1930s, the conservative tendencies of French pronatalism became more pronounced as right-wing reaction to the republic grew in intensity. Populationist rhetoric in the Third Republic also assumed a very anti-modernist tone when focusing on the alleged demise of the family. Pronatalists determined to defend the economic interests of the family in the face of historical change. In this sense, French pronatalism can be characterized as an organized reaction against the modernization which threatened the interests of family agriculture and peasant proprietorship, the symbols of order and stability for successive generations of French populationists. Pronatalism served as an instrument with which the property-owning classes could articulate their demands for protection by the state. Another attribute of French pronatalism which is particularly striking is the pre-eminent role assigned to fathers as saviours of the nation.

French pronatalists all shared the conviction that male heads-of-household should be given special citizen rights and economic privileges. It seems especially noteworthy that evolving welfare policy should continue to weigh on this curious presumption. Scholars of modern France have remarked repeatedly that the actual influence of French pronatalism remained slight throughout much of the period from 1871 to 1945. Although this is true to a certain extent, a widespread pronatalist consensus did become a dominant force in French politics and succeeded in introducing a familist bias in legislation which persisted as a central tenet of the emerging welfare state during the Third Republic. From its inception with the formation of the republic, 'modern' French social policy privileged the family at the expense of other groups, such as the aged and the infirm, which were only belatedly given an equal claim to state benefits. Perhaps decades of lobbying by different pronatalist organizations detrimentally affected the development of those kinds of public provision not targeted at families. The essentially authoritarian and conservative tendencies of French pronatalist politics came to fruition under the Vichy regime. Illustrating just how effective the ideology of the family could be as an instrument of authoritarian rule, Pétain deployed pronatalist familism to mobilize support for his dictatorship.

The attractions of pronatalism for nationalist governments longing to stabilize rule did not go undetected by other dictators. Pronatalist and familist credos contributed to the consolidation of many of the authoritarian regimes of the interwar period. Population programmes which were pro-family, pro-Catholic, anti-abortion and anti-feminist grew in popularity in countries like Italy and France, where religious and social attitudes favouring repressive reproductive politics were strong. Familist nationalism not only served the larger political objectives of the 'New States' which arose in the 1930s, but it also became a defining feature of these regimes. After the destruction of a fledgling republic which survived only from 1910 to 1926, and during which forty-five different governments had tried unsuccessfully to secure parliamentary democracy from the threat of recurring army coups, Portugal fell under the grips of a military dictatorship. The new *ditadura militar* which lasted from 1926 to 1932 proved to be no more stable than the First Republic had been. Increasingly isolated from a base of support, successive senior officers assumed control of governments which clumsily veered from one crisis to another (Gallagher 1981: 325–53). Not until civilian leadership was restored did the Portuguese dictatorship acquire the consistent political programme which was a prerequisite for the achievement of internal stability.

Soon after he acceded to the premiership in 1932, Antonio Salazar, Finance Minister since 1928, launched a patriotic crusade for national regeneration and the restoration of the family as the pillar of Portugese society. Appealing directly to the attitudes and interests of the conservative landowning classes, the military, the industrialists and the Church who gave him their allegiance, Salazar made a socially regressive but mass-mobilizing ideology of family and nation the guiding principle for his *Estado Nôvo*. Borrowing theories of corporatism and totalitarianism from European fascist movements and regimes, Salazar blended these elements into a distinctly Portuguese political Catholicism which espoused belief in the Christianizing role of the authoritarian state. Salazar owed much of his success as a dictator to the attractions of his traditionalist family policy to Portuguese élites. Consolidating what was to become Western Europe's longest dictatorship in the twentieth century, an integral nationalism extolling *Deus, Patria, e Familia* became the basis for a right-wing regime which survived until 1974 (Schmitter 1980: 435–66).

In Brazil too, reproductive politics played a big part in shaping and stabilizing a dictatorship which spanned the years from 1930 to 1945. A military revolt resulted in the collapse of the First Republic in 1930 and the formation of a provisional government under a Junta. After their seizure of power, the insurgents handed the presidency over to their leader, a politician named Getúlio Vargas, who maintained command until 1945, when another military coup occurred. Vargas immediately set out to consolidate his control over the armed forces and the apparatus of the state. In 1934, a new Constitution was issued, one which defined the Brazilian dictatorship as an *Estado Nôvo* committed to recovery from the world depression and reconstruction as a strong and unified nation. Like that of Salazar, Vargas' regime determined to 'reorganize' Brazil along authoritarian lines. At first, the dictator exploited a nationalist party whose nation-wide organization he used to mobilize support for his regime. A variety of Latin American nationalism which shared much in common with European fascism, the Brazilian Integralistas movement formed in 1932 by Plinio Salgado became the institutional foundation for Vargas' dictatorship. Much as Italian fascist ideologues celebrated *Romanità* and borrowed extensively from eugenic theories, integralist nationalists extolled *Brasilidade*, or 'Brazilianness', the quality and essence of the Brazilian 'race'. A form of political pietism, as well as eugenic nationalism, Integralist ideology was also steeped in Catholic doctrine on the family and morality (Griffin 1991: 151).

Vargas' New State placed as much emphasis on a conservative rendition of family politics as did Pétain's Vichy regime. And as he began to assert the autonomy of his regime from the Army and the Integralists, Vargas implemented a population policy which shared much with those of the European dictatorships and democracies. The creation of a new national Department of Health in 1934 was matched by the passage of a series of welfare legislation. Reforms protecting the social security of the family became a political priority, as did a programme of social hygiene to improve the health of the people. Although the regime had difficulty actually implementing its welfarist policy, it moved quickly to approve new laws restricting child and female labour, guaranteeing women maternity services and giving labour statutory rights. As in Europe, race became the prime focus for concern about national identity and the central tenet of population policy. Although Brazil was divided along racial, ethnic, class and regional lines, an official policy of 'Brazilianization' attempted to encourage belief in the existence of one nation. Differences between 'blacks' and 'whites', between rich and poor and between Indians and Europeans were dismissed as irrelevant to the workings of a diverse but harmonious society of 'Brazilians' (Leys Stepan 1990: 138–44).

Under Franco, Spain also implemented a population policy which used Catholicism, pronatalism and nationalism as the ideological trappings for dictatorship. Seeking to integrate the masses into the 'New State', Franco's regime was based on the political myths of a 'national resurrection' through birthrate increase. Beginning in July 1938, only six months after the consolidation of a regime won with 'blood and bayonets' during the Civil War, General Franco's 'National Catholic State' began to introduce French-style pronatalist measures designed to regenerate the race and restore Old Spain. Like Mussolini before him, Franco had a specific target in mind when he committed domestic policy to demographic growth. He wanted the Spanish population to reach forty million inhabitants within a few decades (Del Campo 1974: 491; Nash 1991: 161–3). Just as fascist Italy's birthrate campaign borrowed heavily from the taxation reforms implemented by Third Republic governments, Franco's family policy focused on introducing social insurance and welfare legislation favouring large families. On 18 July 1938, the Franco regime introduced an enactment which centralized the control of a family allowance system that had developed in some industries and made this provision compulsory for all employers. Francoism determined to protect the paternity rights of fathers and to guarantee all families a decent livelihood. In subsequent policies that echoed the aims of Pétain and other statesmen in Europe, the dictatorship increased the severity of punishments against abortion, thereby making the denial of women's reproductive rights one of the cornerstones of the regime. Official propaganda defined the murder of an innocent foetus as a more serious offence than the murder of a sinful person. In the twentieth century, 'the family' became one of the fundamental preoccupations of different states whose leaders officially recognized it as the foundation of society and bestowed it with inalienable rights.

3 Nazi population policy

Pronatalism and antinatalism during the Third Reich

All the human culture, all the results of art, science, and technology that we see before us today, are almost exclusively the creative product of the Aryan.... He is the Prometheus of mankind....

With satanic joy in his face, the black-haired Jewish youth lurks in wait for the unsuspecting girl whom he defiles with his blood, thus stealing her from her people. With every means he tries to destroy the racial foundations of the people he has set out to subjugate.... [But] a racially pure people which is conscious of its blood can never be enslaved by the Jew. In this world he will forever be master over bastards [mixed races].

(Adolf Hitler. From volume 1 of *Mein Kampf*, first published in July 1925)

Scholars have long recognized how central the goal of population increment was to Nazism. As early as 1938, Clifford Kirkpatrick studied the Nazi dictatorship's campaign to increase the birthrate. As in Fascist Italy, party and state in the Third Reich lavished public praise and financial reward on citizens who produced many children for their leader. And like Mussolini, Hitler made health and welfare the pivot of his pronatalist programme. Nazism's new mass institutions for mothers, Kirkpatrick argued, encouraged German women to take pride in the feminine values of motherliness, loyalty and self-sacrifice for family and nation. While acknowledging that National Socialism also sought to breed hatred in women for Jews, Bolsheviks and foreigners, Kirkpatrick focused almost exclusively on the more positive aspects of the regime's population policy (Kirkpatrick 1938). Writing in 1940, however, D. V. Glass did note that the Nazis aimed not at 'unrestricted' but rather at 'racially qualified' demographic growth. The regime pursued a selective pronatalist policy which sought both to encourage 'Aryans' to have large families and to prevent 'non-Aryans' from procreating. But Glass also examined only those legislative measures which were aimed at inducing numerical increase (Glass 1967: 282).

After the liberation of the concentration camps in 1945, historians could no longer ignore the more negative aspects of Nazism. The Holocaust raised all sorts of questions which scholars have since sought to address. The issue of culpability for genocide has figured as a central feature of much of the historical debate. In the immediate postwar period, scholars formulated theories of 'totalitarianism' in order to understand how the unthinkable had happened (Ayçoberry 1981: 127–37). First published in 1951 at the height of the Cold War, Hannah Arendt's brilliant but ultimately flawed account compared the regimes of Hitler and Stalin and concluded that both were based on the 'total domination' of society by the mass-mobilizing, one-party state. What made these twentieth-century and 'modern' dictatorships so different from earlier and other systems of repressive rule, she recognized, was that their leaders and followers were driven by fanatical devotion to the tenets of their ideology, a set of ideas and goals which assumed the mystical character of religious doctrine. She identified a common trait which also distinguished these regimes from conventional capitalist states, what Tim Mason years later called 'the primacy of politics', the relentless and sometimes self-defeating pursuit of political objectives at all costs (Mason 1968: 165–96). 'The aggressiveness of totalitarianism', Arendt wrote, 'springs not from lust for power, and if it feverishly seeks to expand, it does so neither for expansion's sake nor for profit, but only for ideological reasons' (Arendt 1962: 458). In their struggle for world conquest, Bolshevism and Nazism, she argued, both sought empire abroad and ruled with tyranny at home. But their ultimate 'totalitarian' aim, she argued, was to recreate man and woman in their own image, to tamper with evolutionary natural selection, to fabricate a new species by abolishing 'the infinite plurality and differentiation of human beings' (Arendt 1962: 438). A vast 'experiment' in socio-biological engineering, the concentration camps and extermination policies of these states were the outcome of a similar vision which could tolerate no difference and no individuality among the mass of humanity whom they ruled (Arendt 1962: 437–41).

According to Arendt, the incomprehensible 'evil' of the Holocaust had happened because Nazism followed the insane imperatives of its own 'totalitarian' ideology. 'Totalitarianism' in power, she wrote so forcefully, destroyed not just civil rights but also the most sacred of all liberties, the power an individual had over his or her own body and the freedom to choose whether or not to have children. Exterminism was the logical outcome of a form of rule of unequalled barbarity and cruelty, one which rejected outright the principles of the inherent worth of human beings and of the sanctity of life. Following in Arendt's wake, Jacob L. Talmon and others also described the Nazi dictatorship as a ruthless police state wielding an unprecedented amount of power over the German people through rigorous indoctrination backed up by the systematic use of organized terror and violence (Sauer 1967: 404–6). Many postwar accounts also focused on the personality of the dictator. Hitler was seen as an embodiment of evil and the irrational, a tyrant and psychopath driven by a fierce hatred for the Jews and an iron will to destroy them (Bullock 1952). More recently, however, historians began to revise earlier opinions about the seeming totalitarian structure of the Nazi state. Much of the debate in the last twenty years has focused on identifying 'cracks in the monolith'. Hitler's detachment from leadership, decentralized administration, conflicting pressures on government from competing interest groups and endless party rivalry began to dominate discussions in the 1970s of how 'disorganized', 'weak', 'polycratic' and 'chaotic' Nazi rule really was (Broszat 1981; Kershaw 1985). Revisionists argued that there was no malice of forethought behind what they characterized as an unplanned policy to exterminate the Jews. Over fifty years later, we were left more in doubt than ever about who was to blame for mass murder.

The question of how the Holocaust 'fits' into the wider history of the Third Reich has also sparked much controversy. Although some revisionist scholars saw the Final Solution as an accidental 'by-product' of the Second World War, historical research has more recently been published which draws connections between Nazi race and population policies (Browning 1992: ch. 4). Much of this new work of the 1980s emphasized the attributes of Nazi race hygiene, the ideology behind the regime's population programme. Gisela Bock, for example, used the term 'antinatalism' to describe aspects of Nazi policy which aimed at the elimination of 'racial' defects and disease through a vast scheme for enforced selective breeding. In Nazi eugenic thinking, racial defilement through interbreeding with inferior races caused blood pollution. The aim of the Nazi racial state was to purify the 'blood' of the German people by wiping out all contaminants. As Bock rightly pointed out, the Nazis moved quickly to pass a bill for the compulsory sterilization of the mentally and physically disabled in 1933. Together with this 'antinatalist' measure, 'pronatalist' enactments, like the wartime imposition of the death penalty for abortion, were part of a dual strategy for the state control of fertility. 'Compulsory motherhood' for 'valuable' Germans and 'compulsory sterilization' for the 'unfit' were two faces of a Nazi 'body politics' which systematically deprived individuals of reproductive rights and freedoms. The Nazis categorized which types of behaviour and physical characteristics were racially undesirable; and, ultimately, they classified which 'races' deserved to die. The Nazi vision of a healthy New Racial Order, she argued, was based on the dangerous idea of 'hierarchies' of human worth, adherence to which prepared the path for the Final Solution. A state which sterilized its own citizens in the pursuit of a racial Utopia was merely a few small steps away from mass murder. The sterilization programme was but the first stage of an increasingly radicalized racial population policy culminating first in the 'euthanasia' campaign and then in genocide (Bock 1984: 271–96).

New research like that of Bock has shown definitively that Nazi pronatalism cannot be seen in isolation from Nazi antinatalism. Both imperatives are the defining characteristics of a German population policy which was imbued with racism. What distinguishes Nazi population planning is that it sought to create a master race by encouraging Germans of good stock to breed and preventing people of 'little worth' from procreating. But did either pronatalism or antinatalism have primacy in Nazi ideology and policy? To address that question, we should look first to the other fascist dictatorship for a comparison. When compared to the Nazi programme of race hygiene, Mussolini's demographic campaign to halt 'race suicide' seems crudely obsessed with numbers. From the beginning of his struggle for power, Hitler was far more concerned about qualitative racial improvements than about mere population increment. The two fascist regimes had very different ideological orientations.

A preference for 'positive' eugenic remedies for population decline characterized Mussolini's 'battle for the birthrate'. At no time during the liberal or fascist periods did advocacy of exterminism or selectionism gain many followers. Italian fascist pronatalist rhetoric was racialist in outlook, but it remained, moreover, a nationalist ideology favouring the creation of a re-populated New Roman Empire and a New Fascist Italy. Although racism and anti-Semitism had a long history in Italy, they remained politically inconsequential until the fascist period. While scholars have generally ignored the influence of eugenic conceptions of biological race on Italian fascist thinking, they have rightly stressed that the regime was slow to implement a racial policy (Bernardini 1977: 431–53; Michaelis 1978: 120–30). The launch of an aggressive imperialist campaign in Ethiopia in 1935 and the subsequent conquest of empire unleashed the full force of fascist ideas about the supremacy of the Italian *razza*. In 1936, the dictatorship introduced a series of laws against 'miscegenation' to prevent the 'bastardization' of the Italian race through intermingling with the 'inferior' 'coloured peoples' of Africa. And attacks in the press against the alleged Jewish International and the Judaeo-Masonic conspiracy against fascism increased in number and intensity after the Declaration of Empire. Growing political anti-Semitism culminated in 1937 when Italy and Germany formed the Rome–Berlin Axis, an alliance which brought Italian fascist ideology and aims more in line with those of Nazism.

The *Manifesto of Italian Racism* inaugurated a new militantly racist policy in 1938 as the regime sought to preserve the 'purity' of the 'Italic race' by prohibiting interbreeding with Jews and Africans (Preti 1974: 187–207; Robertson 1988: 37–58; Quine 1990: 246–52). Written by prominent eugenic scientists, the manifesto asserted that 'Jews do not belong to the Italian race' and the proud 'Mediterranean' people of Italy were superior to 'Africans' and 'Orientals'. Italians were clearly not 'immune' to racism and anti-Semitism, as some scholars have curiously contended. The Italian Army committed war crimes against ethnic minorities in the ex-Austrian states; and Italy's policies towards the Jews during the Second World War have been aptly described by one historian as a strange blend of 'benevolence and betrayal'. Of the 33,357 Jews who lived under German occupation in Italy after 1943, 6,746 were deported to the death camps and another 303 were murdered on Italian territory (Stille 1988: 333). It has to be said, however, that Italy's wartime record of atrocities compared favourably to those of other West European nations, whose governments, and many of whose people, enthusiastically collaborated in the Holocaust.

Vichy France, for example, sent about 76,000 Jews to their deaths in the East (Marrus 1988: 65–75). Moreover, Michael R. Marrus and Robert O. Paxton have argued persuasively that, far from being a puppet state of the Nazis, Pétain's Vichy regime pursued an anti-Semitic campaign independently of the Germans. No German *diktat* compelled French political leaders to persecute Jews of French and foreign citizenship. Soon after the promulgation of a new constitution in 1940, Pétain's repressive dictatorship moved quickly to deprive native Jews of any rights, confiscate their property and intern many of them in the fifty French-administered concentration camps. The arrests and deportations of Jews which began in the summer of 1942 were, they contend, a brutal continuation of a systematic policy against 'alien Semitic blood' which began in 1940 without Nazi directives (Marrus and Paxton 1981: 241–2). Trains provided by the state railways organized the transportation of Jews, including thousands of children, in cattle wagons known as *trains phantômes*. The inhuman conditions of transport alone accounted for numerous deaths (Webster 1990: 116–19). French collaboration in the Holocaust demonstrates that the Nazi dictatorship was not alone in its pursuit of extremist population policies. A dictatorship eager to arouse nationalist fervour cultivated a homegrown variety of anti-Semitism with deep roots in French society and culture.

Despite the atrocities which resulted from them, Italian racism and anti-Semitism were, by contrast, almost incidental to the dictatorship's population policy before 1936. The comparative insignificance of racism (defined as advocacy of discriminatory treatment based on the belief in the inherent superiority of some 'races' over others) to Mussolini's demographic campaign was evidenced by the fact that before the Declaration of Empire the regime's spokesmen preferred to use the word *stirpe* (stirp or stirps in English) to describe Italians. In both English and Italian, the term *stirpe* is a scientific one first used systematically by Sir Francis Galton, the English mathematician who founded the 'science' of eugenics. Technically, the word means the physical patrimony of a race, the hereditary endowment which was transmitted from the earliest progenitors to all successive generations by means of the germ-cells, the carriers of immutable genetic traits. What made one race distinct from others, according to eugenicists, was a totality of physical and anatomical attributes which remained unchanged through the course of evolution. But significantly, Galton's followers in Italy used the term to denote not just the biological make-up of the race, but also the entire psychic and emotional inheritance of the Italian people. Like the German term *Volk*, *stirpe* is a powerful and resonant word which means much more than just 'the people' (Mosse 1964: 4); *stirpe* signified all that which comprised the unchanging and superior Italian spirit, essence and mentality out of which emerged humanity's greatest achievements, Italian culture and civilization. Preference for the term *stirpe* indicates that both before and during the fascist regime Italian nationalism was folkish, ethnic and cultural rather than racial in outlook. Italian nationalists, including fascists, exalted the national identity of the Italian *Volk* and sought to preserve all those qualities of Italianness that made Italians so noble (Quine 1990: 24). Italian eugenics, then, had given a scientific basis to traditional patriotic sentiment in Italy. Since the *Risorgimento*, nationalist belief had glorified those shared personal traits which bound the disparate Italian people into one unified nation.

Importantly, only after 1936 did the term *razza* begin to appear regularly in the regime's official propaganda and popular media. This ideological shift reflected the abrupt radicalization of conventional chauvinism in a scientific guise into overt racism of a militant variety. After the creation of empire, the regime used scientific notions of *biological* race to justify discriminatory and segregationist policies. But before then, Mussolini and party loyalists had defined race as shared sentiments and attitudes, a common psychic predisposition which found its highest expression in fascist values. The Duce's pronatalist policy before 1936 had sought only to enhance those traits in Italians which made them a virile and warrior people, chief among which was 'fecundity'. The 'battle for births' aimed principally at imbuing the Italian people with a sense of national identity and pride. It was, however, not originally conceived as the instrument of an ideology and policy for racial domination and selective breeding (Quine 1990: 246–52).

Only in 1936 did fascism embrace the idea that Italians should be protected from racial pollution. The dictatorship's new radical racism, however, did not serve as a pretext for the sort of programmatic atrocities, such as sterilization and 'euthanasia', which Nazism committed against the German people. Biological racism was central to Nazi ideology long before the NSDAP seized power in 1933. The imagined 'purity' of the German race became a justification for crimes against those Germans of 'inferior' stock who threatened the 'blood' of the 'chosen' Aryan race with 'contagion'. Mass murder was the ultimate instrument of a Nazi Utopia in which a vast New Germany peopled only by select Aryans would dominate a racially cleansed Europe. Unlike the Italian variant, the National Socialist state possessed both the political will and the power to implement a comprehensive programme of racial hygiene which included specific policies on mass sterilization, 'euthanasia', medical experimentation on human specimens and genocide. Their policies towards the mentally and physically ill, Jews, gypsies, Russian prisoners of war, homosexuals, Communists and all the other categories of people deprived of their humanity demonstrate beyond any doubt that the Nazis gave precedence to 'negative' eugenic measures.

The apparent uniqueness of Nazi race hygiene has led historians to seek explanations about its origins. Scholars of Nazi population policy have engaged in many of the central debates about German history, the most enduring of which concerns the question of continuity and discontinuity from the Second to the Third Reich. Searching for the 'logic' behind historical developments in Germany, Fritz Stern and George L. Mosse identified the rise of a distinct 'Germanic ideology' of the *Volk* which succeeded in pervading all intellectual life by 1914 and eventually triumphed under Hitler (Stern 1961; Mosse 1964). Long before the birth of National Socialism, Stern argued, 'deep national frustrations and cultural discontents' inspired 'nationalist fantasies and utopias, which found ready assent among the German elite'. The goals of this fervent nationalism were 'the revival of a mystical *Deutschtum*' and 'the creation of political institutions that would embody and preserve' the 'peculiar character of the Germans'. When he asked himself 'why so few of the educated, civilized classes recognized Hitler as the embodiment of evil', Stern concluded that the 'long history of the Germanic ideology' predisposed the middle classes to Nazism and 'prepared the path for Hitler to assume power' (Stern 1961: 291–2 and 294). Ostensibly Mosse was not looking for 'precursors' to Nazism in the nationalist literature of the Bismarckian era. He stated quite clearly that he was concerned only to 'describe the context out of which Nazism emerged'. Despite this caution, however, Mosse argued in an even more deterministic way than Stern had done that *völkisch* ideas permeated the culture and society of Imperial Germany and 'led directly to the German catastrophe of our times'. He asserted that discontented élites found in Nazism what they had long desired, a rebirth of German values and the German nation (Mosse 1964: 5–6 and 8).

A weakness of these works was that they portrayed modern German history as an aberration from the course of Western 'civilization'. Mosse, in particular, contended that the 'ideological evolution which led to National Socialism' was 'typically German'. Despite the fact that rabid nationalism arose in other countries too, 'German *völkisch* thought' before 1914, he maintained, not wholly satisfactorily I believe, 'showed a depth of feeling and a dynamic that was not equalled elsewhere'. How did Mosse know that 'the entire German right' and a 'majority of the nation', indeed 'millions of Germans' (in contrast presumably to only a minority of other

Europeans), had responded to the emotive calls of nationalism even before the advent of Nazism (Mosse 1964: 8 and 317)? I would argue that he underestimated the difficulty of measuring the pervasiveness of certain ideas within a culture and of assessing their impact on policies pursued decades later. Any cultural historian will attest to the fact that there is no simple relationship of cause and effect between ideas and politics. When faced with trying to uncover the origins of the 'German catastrophe' that ended in the Final Solution, perhaps the single most challenging problem of modern European history, Mosse contrived a stereotype of the peculiar 'mind' of the German people and the 'character' of the German nation as the explanation. Germany, he alleged, was unique among the nations of Western Europe for having 'repudiated the rationalism of the Enlightenment and the social radicalism of the French Revolution' (Mosse 1964: 316).

Mosse was right to assert that 'the primacy of the ideology of the *Volk*, nature, and race' distinguished Nazism from other varieties of European fascism (Mosse 1964: 315). But in seeking the reasons for this, he devised an interpretation which described an inevitable momentum behind developments in German history from the nineteenth century. Modern Germany had descended from the idealism of the early nationalists to the nihilism of the Nazis in a series of incremental stages. His and other influential works presented certain intellectual traditions, like the racism and anti-semitism of the European Right, as a uniquely 'German problem' caused by the apparent dominance of these unpleasant ideas in a thoroughly 'illiberal' society.

Ralf Dahrendorf approached the question of continuity from a different angle and rejected the search for a 'Germanic ideology' as unhistorical. He preferred instead to examine those features of the social structure and institutions of modern Germany which might have precluded the rise of 'liberal democracy'. But he too proffered a deterministic model which focused on the pathologies and peculiarities of German history. According to Dahrendorf, the survival of the 'feudal dynastic Prussian state' and the old landed élites of 'Junkerdom' into an industrial age prevented the completion of a successful 'bourgeois revolution' leading to gradual democratization. From its inception to its downfall, the Second Reich had been flawed. The coexistence of 'traditional' social and political and 'modern' economic elements in Imperial Germany, he contended, created explosive tensions which ultimately found expression in Nazism (Dahrendorf 1979: 15 and 45). When trying to trace the origins of Nazism from yet another point of view, Karl Dietrich Bracher also pointed to the *Sonderweg*, the 'peculiar path' which Germany seemingly took in the last two centuries (Bracher 1970). Despite the publication by Blackbourn and Eley of a definitive attack on these tendencies in the historiography, scholars in the future will find it no less tempting to 'read history backwards' by looking for premonitions of Nazism in earlier periods (Hauner 1984: 670; Blackbourn and Eley 1984: chs. 6–8).

Many historians have tried to understand the Holocaust, undoubtedly the greatest 'peculiarity' of German history, by examining the culture and politics of the nineteenth century. They have been right to do so since historical phenomena, like Nazism or any other, are influenced by the past. At its best, the continuity thesis points to the prevalence of a whole complex of *völkisch* ideas which undoubtedly influenced Nazi thinking about the purity of blood and race. At its worst, however, the continuity thesis can collapse into a deterministic mode of reasoning, one which traces the apparently steady progression of nineteenth-century ideas into twentieth-century politics. Although it was not their intention to do so, Stern and Mosse did seem to reduce Nazism to little more than the mere agent of a stereotyped authoritarian and 'Germanic' *Weltanschauung* (worldview) which emerged after unification (see also Mosse 1978). In accounting for the origins of the Holocaust, historians must accord Nazism autonomy in the decision-making behind the extermination policy. Furthermore, German history did not develop along a single path in which there were no alternatives to genocide. In reaction to the methodological muddle caused by a too rigid adherence to the continuity thesis, some scholars have been very concerned to avoid describing Wilhelmine Germany as a nation which was already well on the way towards the Final Solution.

One of the most important among these, Paul Weindling has written a great deal about the German eugenics movement whose leaders founded the Race Hygiene Society in 1905. In a massive work published in 1989, Weindling examined the evolution of ideas and policies about population from the Bismarckian to the Nazi period. Quite rightly, he placed this problem within the more generalized context of how different developing nations responded to the challenges of industrialization, imperialism and birthrate decline (Weindling 1989: 1–11 and ch. 1). By doing so, he avoided the temptation to see German history as a 'peculiar path' which 'deviated' from the route to modernity followed by apparently more liberal and democratic societies. But his perspective also raises other problematical issues of interpretation. Weindling was right to urge other scholars to acknowledge that many of the eugenic ideas which informed Nazi ideology were also current in other countries. But this more sophisticated approach still leaves unanswered the question of why other nations which evolved equally militant racist and anti-Semitic agendas did not implement a 'Final Solution'. What, if anything, made Germany unique is not addressed by Weindling. Nor is the problem of the origins of Nazism tackled directly by him.

Indeed, Weindling was mainly concerned to examine eugenics on its own terms. He removed discussion of it altogether from the question of the causes of Nazism. Weindling defined himself as a revisionist seeking to challenge the view that a consensus of reactionary opinion ever existed in Germany during the period from 1870 to 1945. While German *Rassenhygiene* did attract its share of racists, sexists and anti-Semites, he argued, the movement was far more heterogeneous than historians have so far recognized (Weindling 1989: 8). To what extent has there really been a tendency among historians to ignore the plurality of opinion among eugenicists? Weindling himself did not name any particular scholars who he thought were guilty of exaggerating the extent to which racist and extremist views dominated German eugenics, but he would not have found it difficult to find many misconceptions about eugenics in the literature.

Years ago, Kenneth Ludmerer defined eugenics as a 'pseudo-science' whose increasing popularity in the interwar period hindered by decades progress in the 'real' science of genetics (Ludmerer 1972: 2–4). More recently, Allen Chase called eugenics a 'perversion' of scientific knowledge, an 'unscientific' ideology whose central tenet was racism, and a symptom of the intrusion of politics into science (Chase 1980: xvii). And Benno Müller-Hill argued that the rise of 'murderous' science and medicine during the Second Reich was to blame for the crimes committed by the Nazi dictatorship decades later. The rediscovery in 1900 of Mendelian ideas about inheritance paved the way for the immoral misuse of science embodied in the Third Reich's policies to prevent the procreation of 'inferior' races and individuals (Müller-Hill 1988: 7). These and other interpretations reveal that there is still no general agreement among historians about whether eugenics was a 'progressive', 'reactionary', 'pseudo-scientific', 'scientistic' or even 'proto-Nazi' movement. Some scholars do not even seem to be aware of the fact that eugenics was an international movement with many different national varieties in countries outside the 'industrialized and predominantly protestant parts of the western world' (see Bock and Thane 1991: 12 for quote, and Adams 1990: ch. 1 for details about other nations).

Despite the lack of consensus about the nature of eugenics, Weindling did exaggerate the extent to which other scholars have ignored the different strands within eugenics. Sheila Faith Weiss, for example, has identified the existence of a revisionist tendency among West German scholars who began in the 1970s to correct the view of all German eugenicists as right-wing fanatics with a 'blueprint' for genocide (Weiss 1990: 9). One of the great contributions of Weindling has been to bring this revisionism to the attention of an English-speaking audience. Hopefully, he has also finally put to rest the lingering notion that eugenics was mere racism masquerading as science.

In his major work on the topic, Weindling pointed out that a group of student radicals and utopian socialists founded the German Race Hygiene Society because of their desire for progressive reform. One of its founders, Alfred Ploetz (1860–1940) sought to merge Marxism and Darwinism, two intellectual traditions which he believed aimed at the betterment of humankind. Far from being a symptom of militant pan-Germanism, Weindling asserted, eugenics is best seen as an expression of growing concern over the health and welfare of a nation undergoing rapid economic and demographic flux. The novelty of this new 'science' lay in its fusion of evolutionary theory and hereditarian belief into a Social Darwinist ideology founded on the principle that the same 'laws' governed both social and biological change (Weindling 1989: ch. 2).

Industrialization provoked discussion among the educated middle class about the effects of poverty, factory work and urban lifestyles on the mental and physical well-being of the population. Like many of his generation who reached maturity at the turn of the century, Ploetz despised city life and wanted people to live in clean environments with fresh food, air and water. One of his early dreams at medical school was to found a rural community where like-minded free thinkers could live in harmony with nature. He believed avidly that alcohol and tobacco were poisons which damaged both individual health and future generations (Weindling 1989: 63– 76). Early eugenic thinking from the 1890s focused on the need to improve the quality of life under advanced industrial capitalism. Urbanization also created new social problems. Much like British reformers who grew concerned about 'national efficiency' at the turn of the century, German professionals were troubled by what they mistakenly believed to be rising rates of alcoholism, criminality, prostitution and illegitimacy among the residuum of the proletariat population living in crowded urban slums (Jones 1986: ch. 1). Ploetz and the young doctors who formed his circle were committed to *Lebens-reform*, the idea that the masses could be convinced to adopt healthier middle-class lifestyles through abstinence, work, self-discipline, sport and diet (Weindling 1989: 123–9).

Germany also shared the experience of social change which accompanied industrialization in other countries. As elsewhere in the industrialized world, the problem of 'racial degeneration' provoked increasing interest after 1880. The German birthrate, which had been rising throughout much of the nineteenth century, came to a standstill in the 1880s and began to decrease after about 1900. From a peak of 42.6 live births per 1,000 inhabitants in 1876, one of the highest in Europe, the rate dropped to 28.2 by 1912 and continued to do so thereafter (Usborne 1988: 389; 1990: 200). Although the population grew and levels of adult mortality declined, the fall in fertility followed a century of demographic growth and provoked heated debate after 1912, when the worst census results ever were published. Nationalists spoke of the possibility that Germany would follow the path of weaker powers, like England and France, which, in their estimation, had long since lost the struggle to survive. The rapidity of birthrate decline caused widespread anxiety as alarmists warned of impending 'race suicide'. Since evidence suggested that the middle classes routinely used birth control and that an 'abortion epidemic' gripped the nation, worry over the loss of Germany's best and brightest future generations progressively mounted. In a bid to improve living standards which began much earlier but became increasingly perceptible by the 1920s, the working class too showed a marked tendency to limit family size to two or three children (Woycke 1988: 168–9). In 1924–6, when the net reproduction rate reached an all-time low,[1] many believed that the nightmare of 'depopulation' had begun.

Race hygiene grew out of this increasing awareness of the social consequences of economic development. Like movements elsewhere, German eugenics embodied the beliefs that science had discovered the biological laws governing human and social development and that these principles could be used to improve public health. As such, it was an outgrowth of the increasing

---

[1] The net reproduction rate is considered by demographers to be a more reliable index of a population's true replacement potential than the crude birthrate. It is an estimate of the level at which women of childbearing age replace themselves with a new generation of females.

professionalization of science and medicine which occurred during the course of the last century. *Rassenhygiene* was also an institutional expression of the influence of evolutionary and hereditarian thought. As Darwinist ideas infiltrated universities from the 1860s, academics began to see society as an organic entity which could be changed by means of the social application of scientific knowledge. Research into the hereditary causes of illness also convinced doctors that they would be able to eradicate genetic defect and disease from future generations. Scientists made important discoveries about the respective roles that nature and the environment played in human evolution. These developments eventually filtered into the wider society and fed into existent nationalist concern about the prospect of continued progress in the new century. By the 1890s, many levels of German culture and politics were engaged in debate about the quality and quantity of the population.

By the turn of the century, experts from the biomedical sciences were convinced of their duty to safeguard the nation. Though they were not all uniformly racist and reactionary, as Weindling has shown, their objectives were nationalist and their outlook was authoritarian. Their values were those of the German *Bildungsbürgertum* (middle class) and their corporate interest lay in colonizing new areas of research and employment to enhance their own personal and professional status in the wider community (Weindling 1989: 5–10; 1991: ch. 1 and 310–12). More than in any other advanced nation, science and medicine in Germany were major cultural forces with direct links with the state. In the Kaiserreich (the German Empire), the system of social medicine gave these health professionals opportunities to begin to realize their aims of creating a healthy and disciplined social order.

Even before the outbreak of the First World War, many had gained important posts in Imperial Germany's decentralized system of social medicine. A discernible shift towards 'rational' and 'modern' public provision occurred in Germany after 1883, when Bismarck introduced his compulsory sickness insurance scheme. By 1914, German welfare relied on the 'technocratic administration and professional expertise of a scientifically educated medical profession' (Weindling 1989: 2). A less advanced nation like Italy had to wait until the interwar period for a fascist dictatorship to promote 'collectivist' notions of public responsibility for the care of citizens. And the piecemeal process of laying the 'foundations of the welfare state' in Britain spanned the period from 1906, when liberal reforms were first enacted, to 1945, when the Labour Party socialized health services (Thane 1982: pt. 1). But in prewar Germany, the growth in voluntary, municipal, state and national government agencies for health and welfare gave considerable scope for the spread of the new creed of race hygiene.

Before 1914, according to Weindling, those who dominated the eugenics movement were not *völkisch* extremists who believed in German race supremacy. The threat that eugenicists posed to personal freedoms, he argued, did not derive from their political beliefs so much as their increasing social power. Racial hygiene and social biology consolidated a monopoly of control over the public and private apparatus of the welfare state. This institutional leverage provided a firm base from which to promote a gradual acceptance of a broad public health agenda which took racial improvement as its goal. Race hygiene developed strategies for biomedical control over people's lives which were profoundly authoritarian (Weindling 1989: 7–9 and 131). What Weindling does not examine in any depth, however, is the interaction between science and politics from the late nineteenth century. How the pan-Germanists, for example, used eugenic ideas about race to justify their militarist, anti-Semitic and nationalist programme does deserve some mention. Equally, Weindling does not explore the question of whether eugenic aims, in both their benign and sinister forms, had influenced the thinking of politicians from all parties by 1914. We are repeatedly told by him that the Nazis expropriated the more vehement and extremist strands within eugenics, but we are left uninformed about what political leaders before Hitler believed was the best way to improve the German race.

Weindling also underplayed to some extent the attractions of so-called 'negative' eugenics to German eugenicists. Already in the prewar period, some German eugenicists favoured the adoption of antinatalist measures to curb the reckless over-breeding of 'inferior' individuals. In 1910, the official programme of the German Race Hygiene Society called for immediate legislation to support large families through economic perquisites and to protect mothers and children through welfare benefits. But the movement also sought to wipe out hereditary 'racial poisons' like syphilis, tuberculosis and alcoholism. In addition to their pronatalist objectives, the society endorsed the principle of sound 'selective breeding' and advocated the introduction of marriage restrictions for the biologically 'unfit' and 'work colonies' for the temperamentally 'unproductive' (Weiss 1990: 23). Nor were these relatively moderate proposals the only ones contemplated by German eugenicists.

At the first international conference on eugenics in London in 1912, a small but vocal group of delegates set the proceedings astir by giving papers endorsing 'negative' eugenic measures. Among these were representatives from the self-styled 'Nordic' wing of the international movement who advocated preventive measures to safeguard the race from the transmission of injurious inheritance. German eugenicists sought both to distinguish their version of race hygiene from other national varieties of eugenics and to build closer alliances among the 'Nordic' nations of Holland and Scandinavia. In her address at the 1912 congress, Agnes Bluhm, a physician and eugenicist from Berlin, spoke about the importance of a 'race consciousness' to the medical profession. She urged doctors to reconsider their ethical stance on such controversial matters as the right of the unborn foetus to life. Obstetricians who performed emergency caesarians to save an infant in distress, she argued, failed to recognize that such interventions merely resulted in the birth of a 'crippled imbecile of a child' and a severe liability to the race. The imperative of racial health, she believed, took precedence over any outmoded moral precepts. Weak and degenerate babies, whether they be premature or not, were destined to lead worthless lives as burdens on their families and the state (Bluhm 1912: 387–95).

Just how widespread was this belief in the benefits of 'euthanasia' among prewar German eugenicists and other nationalists? It is an important question since, interestingly, no similar endorsement was given at the 1912 conference by delegates from Italy or France, two nations which showed a marked preference for 'positive' eugenic measures in their population policies. One reason for this divergence of opinion, no doubt, came from the dominance of hereditarian belief among the Germans and the prevalence of environmentalist ideas among the French and Italians. Unlike their colleagues in 'Latin' and Catholic countries, German eugenicists were never firm believers in the goals of welfare reform and birthrate increase. They were far more interested in wiping out hereditary defects by medical means than they were in promoting public health through social policy.

Despite the spread of ideas about national health and efficiency, the actual influence of German race hygiene on prewar social legislation was limited. Prepared in the period 1908 to 1913, a draft penal code contained harsher guidelines on abortion and contraception than those in the 1871 version. The new penal code, however, did not get voted through parliament because of political stalemate in the Reichstag and the outbreak of the First World War. As in other countries, however, the war proved to be a major turning point for the population question in Germany. Both the Reich government and several *Länder* (states) made tentative moves towards implementing a population policy during the mobilization. The most important 'positive' wartime welfare measure was a December 1914 act granting a mandatory maternity benefit to expectant women and new mothers whose husbands were soldiers. Because of the very high mortality rates of 'illegitimate' babies in their first year, these allowances were also given to single mothers in 1915 (Weindling 1989: 268).

Concern over the quality, as well as the quantity, of children being born intensified during the war. The health and welfare of the German populace deteriorated dramatically after 1915 as the government proved increasingly unable to guarantee even the bare minimum of subsistence to its citizens on the home front. Mothers went without milk for their children, rates of infant and child mortality increased, and levels of adult illness and death also rose as war-related hardship and hunger took its toll on the German civilian population (Feldman 1966: 97–115). To offset some of the worst effects of food scarcity, epidemic disease, strict rationing and bread riots after 1916, the state expanded social welfare for infants, children and mothers. To facilitate the growth of 'family-care' relief services, the government forged new links between women's charitable organizations and municipal welfare agencies. Wartime social policy sought to stimulate the birthrate, decrease morbidity and mortality and guarantee domestic cooperation with the war effort.

The Reich also showed a new willingness to introduce reforms with an additional preventive social hygienic purpose. The provision of tax relief for large families, pay rises for factory workers and state employees and better public housing for the poor aimed both at improving the quality and increasing the quantity of the German population. A national network of free venereal disease clinics funded by government insurance offices arose during the war. In addition, the centralization of hospital services and public health administration extended access to and broadened the range of medical care (Weindling 1988: 417–38). *Socialhygiene* as a form of collectivized medicine became an acceptable part of government policy during the war.

But these initiatives never amounted to a comprehensive population policy. Family allowances to married male workers, for example, escaped public regulation during the war. Introduced voluntarily by a few municipal authorities and private industries as early as 1905, the system still covered only limited categories of salaried employees and left the overwhelming majority of factory workers unprotected. Despite sharp price rises during the war which increased the cost of living, and proposals to use child allowances as a pronatalist measure, the Wilhelmine state failed to extend the system of wage bonuses or make the income supplements scheme compulsory. Finance ministers proved reluctant to endorse costly legislation which would necessitate decreased profits for industry (Vibart 1926: 42–7).

Despite the haphazard development of welfare provision, the war did mark a major shift in the relations between state and society. The need to coordinate the civilian mobilization expanded the social domain of the state. Women and children became objects of social policy since they replaced male workers in factories and family life was disrupted. New forms of intervention based on the regulation of reproduction and sexuality also gained acceptance. The 1871 penal code did not criminalize the manufacture and sale of birth control information and devices. In 1917, the Bundesrat (the federal council of the Empire's twenty-five member states) and a select committee of the Reichstag (the German parliament) approved the draft of a proposal to ban the trade in contraceptives and abortifacients. And in 1918, the Bundesrat also passed a bill aiming to halt the apparent rise in abortions and voluntary sterilizations by limiting the right of doctors to perform these for health reasons. Neither of these measures became law because of the political turmoil which accompanied the end of the war (Usborne 1988: 390–1), but they both demonstrate to what extent politicians of all parties were coming around to the idea that the national interest in increasing births was paramount to personal freedoms.

In the immediate postwar period from 1918 to 1924, plans for national reconstruction were intertwined with strategies for the *Socialhygiene* of the war-weary German people. The Republic introduced female suffrage in 1918 and enshrined notions of social justice and equal rights for men and women in its constitution of 1919. During demobilization, the care of soldiers, orphans and widows became a big issue. Officials grew alarmed at statistics showing how malnourished and sickly the war generation were. New cries for immediate state action to stop the 'epidemics' of abortion, birth control, illegitimacy and venereal disease were heard. After the war, the population lobby diversified as citizens' and religious groups of activists appeared on the scene. Numerous private and voluntary middle-class societies devoted to single-issue campaigns for the 'purity of German blood', the 'preservation of the family' and the 'defence of public morality' arose. These included the *Reichs-bund der Kinderreichen Deutschlands zum Schutze der Familie*, a pronatalist and familist organization founded in 1919 which boasted as many as 700 local chapters by 1926. The National League of 'Child-Rich' Families, like its counterparts in France, was a pressure group which lobbied government for special legislation and privi-leges for large families (Stephenson 1979: 351–75). Other associ-ations, such as the conservative League for the Protection of Mothers (*Bund für Mütterschutz*), which was first founded in 1904, enjoyed greater popularity after the war (Taylor Allen 1985: 423; Koonz 1987: 35–6). Others, like the League to Increase and Sustain National Vitality and the League for Regeneration intensified their campaigns and increased their membership. The proliferation of women's, pronatalist and nationalist organizations testified to the pervasiveness of concern over the quantity and quality of the German population.

The hyper-inflation of the years 1922 to 1923 temporarily halted efforts at postwar reconstruction as management of the economic crisis became a government priority. Since domestic consumption of basic necessities plummeted, the high cost of living made the whole problem of health and welfare more urgent. In the 1920s, and especially during the recovery and boom of 1925 to 1928, the Repub-lic gained the requisite political stability and social peace for con-certed population planning. A policy emerged which was pronatalist and welfarist in nature. This period of prosperity saw the expansion of insurance coverage, social services and medical facilities. Success-ive enactments extended the provision of maternity benefit, child welfare, public health, poverty relief and worker compensation.

A distinguishing feature of Weimar social policy was the extent of women's participation in its formation. Inter-party women's groups pressed parliament for progressive legislation. Women's growing political influence was felt in their renewed struggle for a 'New Morality' based on the idea of 'voluntary motherhood' and women's enjoyment of sexual freedom (Melching 1990: 69–85). In 1926, the government cautiously liberalized the abortion laws by reducing the severity of sentences for women and abortionists and by making abortion a misdemeanour when not performed for financial gain. Though not a fundamental change, the new law was a step in the right direction. And given the opposition of the Roman Cath-olic Centre Party and the German National Party, its passage was a remarkable achievement for socialists and communists who supported the principle of women's rights to abortion on request during the first three months of pregnancy. In 1927, the German Supreme Court ruled that abortion for medical reasons was legal if pregnancy posed a danger to the woman's life. This decision laid the basis for a wide interpretation, a consequence of which was the creation of abortion clinics throughout rural and urban Germany. Even after the introduction of these reforms, however, courts continued to convict those who procured and performed illegal abortions (David *et al.* 1988: 84–5).

Another impressive enactment was the 1927 Maternity Protection Act which singled out Germany as one of the first nations to endorse the International Labour Organization's rulings on the rights of women workers (Stoehr 1991: 228). Municipal and federal governments joined in national initiatives to consolidate the welfare state and develop policies which were responsive to the needs of an emergent social democratic society. Birth control clinics providing cheap contraceptives to the working class opened up in many cities. Trade unionists, feminists and socialists lent their support to a massive reform effort which made the German system of nationalized welfare one of the most advanced of its day (Weindling 1989: 342–78).

The Wall Street Crash of October 1929 brought the Republic's social experiment to an end. After the resignation of Weimar's last social democratic coalition government, a right-wing Catholic became Chancellor in March 1930. Brüning's handling of the economic and financial crisis was poor. The basis of his recovery policy, tax increases, wage reductions and budget cuts proved to be misguided at a time when over six million people were unemployed. As foreign capital disappeared and national resources shrank, welfare programmes and social insurance benefits were drastically reduced.

The impact of the depression was most profoundly felt on perceptions of the welfare state. Badly hit by tax hikes, loan recalls and business bankruptcies, the propertied middle classes became much more receptive to the ideas of 'negative' eugenics. Industrialists called for massive restraints on public expenditure and state subsidies for industry. Commentators calculated the costs of custodial care for the various categories of 'welfare dependents', such as the incurably ill, the aged and the insane. The German public, they argued, paid for the upkeep of about 400,000 'congenital idiots', schizophrenics, manic depressives, epileptics, paupers, pensioners and others who were a huge burden on society (Folsom 1934: 264). Financial arguments that Germany could ill afford to maintain a 'surplus' population of people 'of little worth' gained many new adherents.

Race hygienists joined in the chorus of critics who applauded the collapse of the Weimar welfare state. They supported the principle that welfare should not be a universal right of all citizens, but rather should be targeted only at those who contributed to the creation of national wealth. Even before the depression, some eugenicists had endorsed the idea that the physically unfit and mentally unsound should be sterilized in order to prevent them from passing their defective inheritance on to future generations. From the 1890s, arguments in favour of so-called 'voluntary' sterilization focused particularly on the benefits the institutionalized insane could enjoy under a new mental health system. Psychiatric patients would no longer need to be segregated from society if they agreed to be sterilized before release from hospital. At the same time, some medical and legal experts began to support publicly proposals for so-called 'mercy-killing' which they presented as a humanitarian response to a patient's intolerable suffering. They argued that the terminally ill should be given a dignified death rather than be left to lead a 'worthless life' (Weindling 1989: 388–93). In 1922, German race hygienists officially endorsed the principle of the 'voluntary' sterilization of the 'unfit' (Noakes 1984: 82).

German supporters of eugenic sterilization were not alone. Founded in 1907, the English Eugenics Education Society, like their German counterparts, initially advocated an extension of the system of segregation and confinement of the mentally ill. They pressured the government into passing the 1913 Mental Deficiency Act and the amendment to it in 1927, enactments which gave local authorities broad powers to commit the 'hereditarily' ill to indefinite detention. Institutionalization was seen as a 'preventive' hygienic measure which, ideally at least, forced inmates of insane asylums to lead celibate lives. But English eugenicists opposed the Poor Law and many of the statutory and universal social security measures introduced by successive governments (Searle 1976: 64 and 93–112). In the interwar period, they also mounted a very public but ultimately unsuccessful campaign to convince parliament to legalize what they too called the 'voluntary' sterilization of the 'feebleminded' (Macnicol 1989: 147–71; Soloway 1990).

Advocates of 'voluntary' sterilization clearly sought to impose compulsion although they were reluctant to admit to this for fear of attracting opposition to such a controversial issue. Use of the term 'voluntary' served their purposes by giving the impression that mental patients might actually be able to exercise free choice or give informed consent. By means of propaganda and pressure, campaigners wished to bring the government and the public around to the idea that society should sterilize those with an injurious inheritance. Supporters of sterilization, both in England and in Germany, always hastened to point out that their motives were purely humane. But the élitism and class prejudice behind their proposals did not go unnoticed by critics. Unlike their Italian colleagues, German and English eugenicists shared a pronounced disdain for the working class. Middle-class experts in these countries sought to educate a 'respectable' middle-class public about the dangers of racial defilement by the degenerate proletariat. Since organized campaigns for sterilization arose just as the welfare state expanded, financial considerations undoubtedly influenced scientific opinion.

Growing acceptance of the idea of sterilization on eugenic grounds was one symptom of the increasing radicalization of politics in postwar Germany. Germany's humiliating experience of defeat and the harsh terms of the peace settlement provoked a defensive nationalist response which found expression in the gradual mobilization of the racialist Right. Dissatisfaction with the progressive welfare policies of the Weimar regime propelled many to embrace the idea of 'selective' welfare and breeding. In July 1932, the Committee for Population Questions and Eugenics of the Prussian State Council of Health unanimously endorsed a number of proposals for a racial population programme which included a bill on the 'voluntary' sterilization of the hereditarily unfit. The German Medical Association warmly welcomed these deliberations (Noakes 1984: 84–5). In the same month, the Nazis attracted 37.4 per cent of the vote in a general election which crowned their record of success at the polls and paved the way for Hitler's appointment as Chancellor in January. While historians have traditionally focused on the economic causes for the collapse of the Weimar Republic, social factors undoubtedly had their part to play. Both before and during the depression, the growing strength of the New Right was based on the broad appeal of their platform. Organized and militant racism of many varieties increasingly found recruits among the swollen ranks of those discontented with social democracy. The growing popularity of right-wing policies on population and race were a bitter condemnation of the principles of social justice and equal rights encoded in the Weimar constitution.

Nazi ideology combined *völkisch* racism with extremist eugenics. In *Mein Kampf*, Hitler outlined the tenets of the National Socialist idea of a racial state predicated on purity of blood and physical health. The mission of National Socialism, he explained, was to preserve the superiority of the Aryan race by preventing cross-breeding with lower species. Hitler greatly admired the American immigration acts of 1921 and 1924 because these blocked the entry of undesirable 'aliens' by means of strict racial and ethnic quotas. America could boast to be a racist state since its laws severely restricted the flood of Slavic, Jewish, Mediterranean and Asiatic peoples from the Far East and Europe. Only full-blooded white immigrants from 'Anglo-Saxon' and 'Nordic' countries were allowed to enter the United States in large numbers. The *völkisch* state, Hitler affirmed, abrogated all those detestable civil freedoms on which weak and degenerate democratic states were based. According to him, marriage was a lasting union of genetically healthy persons of the same race and different sexes who came together in order to perpetuate the race and nation. In the New Nazi Order that he hoped to create, legal and medical sanctions would prohibit the hereditarily ill and the racially inferior from breeding (Hitler 1969: 358–98; Weindling 1989: 490–2; Burleigh and Wipperman 1991: 37–43).

Nazi ideology was based on the idea that the state was the highest social form, the embodiment of the people, race, and nation and everything, including the rights of individuals to marry and pro-create, was subordinated to its sovereign interest (Hitler 1969: 524). Nazi leaders put this belief into practice by implementing the most 'totalitarian' of all those racial population programmes of the inter-war period. Health and race formed the core of Nazi thinking about population. The Third Reich retained the basic structure of social welfare which had been strengthened under the Weimar Republic. But the NSDAP leadership used this system of social security and welfare to further their own distinct political agenda. The Nazis shifted the focus of policy from social hygiene towards race hygiene and aggressively pursued racial perfection.

The Nazi party in power established the principle of racial selec-tion in all legislation and launched selective welfare policies discrimi-nating against the 'unfit' and 'inferior'. The Nazis supported racialized notions of the welfare state which dictated that only true Aryans could enjoy benefits which aimed at helping them rear healthy children. The regime rapidly withdrew the universal rights to welfare encoded in the Weimar constitution and restricted the access of Jews to employment and benefits. Health and welfare provision was seen as a means to create a powerful new German people, cleansed of all racial poisons and foreign contaminants.

Because of its greater resources, the Nazi party also took a more activist role in welfare activities than did the Fascist party in Italy. The NSDAP usurped the function of traditional private charities and politicized the role of social welfare by imbuing it with a racialist political purpose.

The dictatorship determined to reverse the trend of birthrate decline by vigorous pronatalist policies. As in other countries struggling with the problem of 'race suicide', Nazi propaganda focused on the importance of women to its demographic campaign. The Nazis insisted that men and women had separate roles and that the primary function of females was to reproduce the race. According to them, the feminist movement was an invention of Jewish radicals who conspired to destroy the *Volk* by undermining traditional values and the 'natural' hierarchy between the sexes on which German society was based. The idea that politics was the exclusive domain of men was reflected in party membership. Despite the fact that women voters had comprised a significant source of electoral support, female membership in the party comprised no more than 6 per cent of the total in 1933. And while Weimar's left-wing parties had put a record number of women in parliament, the Nazi party had no female deputies. As in fascist Italy, mass organization and segregation by sex became a priority for a state committed to training women to become good wives and mothers.

The dictatorship sought to integrate all social institutions in the new state. The regime absorbed existing Protestant women's organizations and created the *Deutsches Frauenwerk* (The German Women's Bureau) in 1933. The Bureau gave the Nazis a powerful instrument of political penetration and persuasion. The Nazis conceived the Bureau as a huge service corps where women would learn to perform their highest duty towards the state, the care of their families. With a membership of between four and six million, depending on the source, the *Frauenwerk* had an institutional presence throughout rural and urban Germany. The activities of female members were restricted to the so-called traditional womanly and motherly pursuits of knitting, sewing and cookery, and all classes were run by party activists. The organization created Mothers' Schools which offered courses in household management and baby care. Membership was given only to those of proven Aryan stock who supported the regime. Worthy entrants also received Nazi indoctrination in 'racial science courses' aimed at inculcating hatred towards Jews, Bolsheviks and foreigners. The organization attempted to convert women to the new Nazi faith and to inspire in them a loyalty to the nation, the Führer, the state and the race (Noakes and Pridham 1984: 452; Koonz 1987: 245–53).

Another source of propaganda and control was the Nazi Mother and Child Organization, which was accountable to the party's welfare service. By 1938, the Nazis claimed to have created 25,000 racial health centres where over ten million women had gone for eugenic advice (Noakes and Pridham 1984: 452). Also inspired by measures introduced by Mussolini's regime, as well as those of democratic states, the Nazi leadership issued the Mother's Cross to particularly prolific women as a medal of honour for their patriotic service to the Third Reich. Female party members with many children were also encouraged to wear special fertility runes on their uniforms as signs of distinction (Kudlien 1990: 234–6). These motifs reflected the general militarization of civil society promoted by a regime which mobilized women to fight Germany's 'War of Births'.

The Nazis introduced many other procreative incentives. They increased maternity benefits and income tax allowances for dependent children. Following the example of other countries, they gave large families reduced fares on public transport. They also expanded the existing voluntary system of family allowances which hitherto had benefited mainly civil servants. The government's sponsorship of new equalization funds slightly increased the number of industries and professions which offered such wage supplements. But the Nazis never showed any great commitment to making family allowances a compulsory scheme covering all workers with dependent children. Purportedly designed to reduce child poverty, the Third Reich's family allowance scheme was a failure, since so few new workers gained entitlement. And given the paltry amount of the subsidies offered, it could never have provided parents with much incentive to have large families. The Nazi system compared unfavourably with the more extensive French version on which it was modelled (Glass 1967: 293–5).

The Nazis were particularly proud of their marriage loan system, however. They claimed it was a 'positive' pronatalist measure which was both generous and effective. Created in 1933, the loan system was part of a government initiative to quicken the pace of the recovery from depression by reducing levels of male unemployment. The scheme gave couples interest-free loans of up to 1,000 marks whose repayment was cancelled when they had their fourth child. Issued in the form of coupons for household goods, the loans were initially given on condition that the future wife who had worked for at least six months previous to her wedding give up gainful employment after marriage (Mason 1976: pt. I, 95–6). The fund to pay for the loans was partly financed by the revenue from a 'celibacy tax' on unmarried men and women inspired by similar French legislation. Estimates do vary, but as many as just over a million couples received a loan from 1933 to 1938. Because the great majority of loans were cancelled due to couples having four children or more, the regime proclaimed them to be a great success (Glass 1967: 287–92). Their impact was no doubt greater than that of the rather cosmetic loan scheme launched by the Vichy dictatorship in 1940 as part of its ruralization programme. But historians have cast doubt on the effectiveness of this form of pronatalist measure.

The German marriage rate did increase during the Third Reich and the Nazis attributed this to the impact of loans. Accounting perhaps for the immediate rise in 1934 and subsequent years, the scheme may have given some encouragement to working-class and lower middle-class people who had deferred marriage during the economic crisis which began in 1929. But how many of these marriages would have taken place without the benefit of loans is a matter of some speculation. The actual effect of the loans on family income was limited. The cost of raising children was not substantially offset by the amount of the financial aid provided by the loan, even with its cancellation. The shortcomings of other aspects of Nazi policy also belie the claim that the dictatorship gave working parents real economic incentives to produce more children. The government promised but failed to increase the availability of cheap public housing in the cities. And the regime's management of the economy created price inflation which adversely affected the household budgets of working-class families. Most probably, the rise in the marriage rate was caused by the end of the turmoil of the depression years. The relative stability of the 1930s, rather than Nazi initiatives themselves, might account for the apparent willingness of more people to marry (Kudlien 1990: 235).

The birthrate also increased from fifty-nine live births per 1,000 women of childbearing age in 1932 to seventy-seven in 1934. The rate remained the same until 1938 when it rose to eighty-one and continued to do so until 1940. But Nazi population policy did not seriously tackle the problem of infant mortality, particularly that of first-years, which remained remarkably high for such an economically advanced nation. Neither did Nazi pronatalism reverse the long-term trend towards fertility decline. Quite rightly, Jill Stephenson has pointed out that the German birthrate underwent a period of stabilization during the Nazi era. Other countries, for example

Italy, also experienced brief upturns in the interwar period. These occurred, most notably, immediately after the First World War and the Great Depression. After three decades of rapid decline, the German birthrate experienced a modest but temporary rise. And the upswing, she argued, only seems dramatic when figures for the Nazi period are compared to those for the depression years when the birthrate reached an all-time low. When set against the highs of the previous century, or even 1920s' levels, the Nazi achievement seems rather slight (Stephenson 1979: 367–9). Presuming that the official statistics are reliable, this argument still does not discount the possibility that Nazi policies were directly or even partly responsible for this shift. However, any interpretation is problematical given the difficulty of generalizing about people's attitudes towards childbearing from aggregate demographic data.

Whether the rise in births was attributable to positive incentives or punitive measures is also a matter of debate. The Nazis introduced some of the most severe legislation against abortion and birth control in all of Europe. In May 1933, they fulfilled their election promise to make these 'crimes against the race' which were punishable by a maximum sentence of penal servitude for fifteen years. Increasingly harsh restrictions placed on the availability of contraception and on access to legal abortion culminated in the wartime creation of special courts, like those in Vichy France, with powers to impose the death penalty for the treasonable offence of procuring, inducing or performing an illegal termination. Unlike the French courts, which carried out their mandate only once, surviving Nazi archives seem to indicate that a number of lay women who were convicted of being abortionists were executed during the war (David *et al.* 1988: 95–7).

Cornelia Usborne makes the important point that repressive laws of this nature could not work since most people used the withdrawal method of birth control and most abortions were self-induced (Usborne 1988: 400–6). But with regard to the policing of abortionists, both medical and lay, the Nazis were brutally efficient. Prosecutions and convictions for this crime increased dramatically during the Third Reich, although the number of illegal abortions performed annually apparently also rose (David *et al.* 1988: 93). Nazi repression put sympathetic midwives and doctors who performed abortions in grave danger. And the atmosphere of extreme antipathy towards abortion might have convinced some women who were already in doubt for religious or personal reasons to carry their babies to term.

As part of their plan to improve the quality of the German people, the Nazis implemented a policy of race hygiene. Welfare benefits were to be given only to those who met Nazi criteria of being mentally and physically fit. Forms of 'asocial' behaviour such as alcoholism, single motherhood and prostitution were deemed to be genetically determined. These and a host of other supposedly congenital diseases were to be eliminated. A law to prevent the birth of hereditarily sick children by means of sterilization was quickly promulgated in July 1933. A redraft of a Prussian bill prepared in 1932, which adhered to the specious principle that doctors should only carry out 'voluntary' procedures after the 'consent' of a patient or his or her parents, family or guardian had been granted, the new law made no pretence of the fact that sterilization would now be compulsory. The Third Reich's legislation stated that anyone who had an inheritable illness could be rendered sterile if there was a strong probability that his or her offspring would suffer from physical or mental defect. The illnesses classified as hereditary included chronic alcoholism, feeblemindedness, schizophrenia, manic depression, epilepsy, Huntington's chorea, blindness, deafness and physical deformity. The responsibility for a sterilization order lay with the district Hereditary Health Court which comprised a magistrate, a medical officer and another physician. The law empowered doctors to report their suspicions about any patient to the local health court. The residing medical officer would then issue a sterilization order if the patient could not be 'persuaded' to 'request' a procedure (Noakes 1984: 86).

There was nothing particularly 'Nazi' or 'fascist' about the Third Reich's sterilization programme. Inspiration for it came from the United States where overtly compulsory sterilization found its way into state law in 1907, when Indiana passed a bill ruling that surgeons could 'de-sexualize' the 'degenerate' on eugenic grounds. But even before then, operations were performed without benefit of statute. The first known case was reported in Pennsylvania where a superintendent at a home for deficient children castrated a teenage boy in 1889. The child was found to have a 'sad inheritance' which predisposed him to 'wanderlust, alcoholism, low mentality, thievishness, sexual perversion, and other defects'. Physicians considered sterilization to be a cure for insanity, criminality and all the allegedly terrible consequences of masturbation in adolescents. In 1905, both houses of the Pennsylvania legislature approved a law preventing 'idiocy' in children by means of compulsory sterilization. Despite a veto by the state's governor, sterilizations continued there for decades thereafter and most of the victims were mentally retarded boys in the care of the state (Landman 1932).

The legality of compulsory sterilizations remained in doubt until 1927, when the Supreme Court reviewed a 1925 State Supreme Court ruling permitting sterilization on eugenic grounds. The case under review involved an appellant who, like her mother before her, was committed to a colony for epileptics and the feebleminded in Virginia. Found to be of 'sub-normal intellect', she was recommended for sterilization after her daughter was tested at the age of one month and was also diagnosed to be a carrier of 'inferior intelligence'. The presiding judge, Oliver Wendell Holmes, made a landmark decision to uphold the constitutionality of compulsory sterilization. Chief Justice Holmes revealed the thinking behind his questionable judgement on the case when he remarked that 'three generations of imbeciles are enough'. He affirmed that the state had the right to require those citizens who were economic and social burdens on society to make 'lesser sacrifices' for the greater good (Duster 1990: 29–30).

By the 1930s, thirty-two states in the union permitted what doctors dispassionately referred to as 'sexual mutilation' or 'sexual amputation'. The number of compulsory sterilizations increased continually precisely because they never became part of a central government policy which could arouse public opposition. The fact that they were carried out on the most vulnerable members of society, those institutionalized in state and charitable care facilities, gave this form of medical policing a relative 'invisibility'. Remarkably few appeals ever came before the courts despite the fact that institutions were not required to get the consent of parents or guardians. As critics pointed out, the relatives of persons committed to prisons or asylums were frequently not even told of the operation beforehand. And many of the victims who were orphaned or abandoned children would have been 'wards of the court' with no means to oppose the measure. Medical officers compiled what they called a 'hereditary family history' and performed the operation based on whether evidence of a particularly harmful pedigree was found. Informed parents who objected could seldom afford legal representation. The immigrant, the poor and the mentally ill comprised the vast majority of those who were compulsorily sterilized, and more women than men figured among the victims. Class, race, gender and ethnicity, more than sound medical diagnosis, determined whether a person would be classified as a moron and recommended for sterilization (Folsom 1934: 263).

Although they continued for decades after 1945, the bulk of American sterilizations were performed in the 1930s, when the Nazis were also persecuting individuals in the guise of psychiatry. The introduction of compulsory sterilization is such an important issue precisely because this violation of an individual's integrity epitomizes an extreme in a state's 'totalitarian' control over the body. Because of this, historians have suggested that once the Nazis began to implement their mass sterilization programme, they were well on their way towards the Final Solution (Mosse 1978; Lifton 1986; Weindling 1989 and others). While no scholar has argued that the Holocaust which began in 1942, or even the 'euthanasia' campaign which commenced in 1939, was an inevitable outcome of earlier initiatives against the Jews specifically or against 'asocials' and the 'hereditarily ill', there is wide recognition of the progressive erosion of moral standards, medical ethics and liberal values which the dictatorship caused. The regime coordinated and nazified all health professionals and gave them the authority to implement a biological politics based on racial selection. The sterilization policy marked the first stage of an incremental process of radicalization as the Third Reich moved feverishly towards the creation of a new racial order. On a philosophical and moral level, the difference between sterilization and murder on eugenic grounds is one of degree only, as both are predicated on the belief that individual rights and human life have no inherent worth.

The American example disproves this thesis to a certain extent. The United States never made any jump from mass sterilization to mass murder despite the presence of a eugenic lobby, such as the Euthanasia Society, with decidedly dangerous views (Kevles 1985: 108–12). Liberal-democratic institutions in America may have provided some obstacle to the realization of plans for the 'merciful release' of patients with incurable illnesses. However, even this interpretation is subject to qualification since the legality of compulsory sterilization was upheld by the highest court in the land despite the rights to due process and equal protection given to all citizens by the Constitution. The rule of law in a liberal democracy did not prevent this clear violation of constitutional guarantees from happening. And the point remains that in both a dictatorship and a democracy, the belief in the sanctity of human life and the inviolability of the body was under attack.

To counterbalance this argument, historians have argued that what distinguished the Nazi sterilization programme from others was its scale and impact. Figures convey just how far-reaching was the Nazi programme, one which aimed at sterilizing as many as 20 per cent of the German people. One count of the toll of the Nazi programme is that about 200,000 people were sterilized between 1933 and 1937, of whom 102,218 were men and 95,165 were women (Noakes 1984: 87; Noakes and Pridham 1984: 458). By 1945, the number reached an estimated 360,000, totalling about 1 per cent of the German population (Weindling 1989: 533). The figures most cited by scholars maintain that only about 12,145 compulsory sterilizations were performed in the United States in the period from 1907 to 1932 (Noakes and Pridham 1984: 458). But estimates of the impact of both programmes vary wildly (see, for example, Marrus 1988: 52; Soloway 1990: 309). Some accounts maintain that many thousands of sterilizations of mental retardates went unrecorded in Germany in the 1930s because they were done secretly (Lifton 1986; Fleming 1986). And more reliable figures for the United States hold that out of a cumulative 64,000 during the period 1907 to 1963, when these statutes were revoked, about 45,000 were compulsorily sterilized in the years 1927 to 1945 alone (Blacker 1962: 155–6; Reilly 1977: 126). But even these figures cannot be considered to be an accurate reflection of the real numbers of inmates in penal and psychiatric establishments who were involuntarily sterilized. How many operations went unrecorded is simply not known. Importantly too, many effectively compulsory procedures were also performed in the United States under the guise of different rulings on 'voluntary' sterilization.

Eugenically-minded American doctors believed that as much as 30 per cent of the population suffered from some 'neuropathic taint' which was transmittable to their offspring. In these cases, they advocated treatment by means of the removal of both testicles in men. Although vasectomy was less surgically aggressive than this, doctors preferred castration since it was irreversible. On women, they performed a salpingectomy (removal of the Fallopian tubes), ovariotomy (removal of the ovaries) or hysterectomy (removal of the uterus), and just to be sure, occasionally all three operations (Van Wagenen 1984: 465–70). They too wanted to sterilize on a mass scale, arguing that anything less would leave tens of thousands of people to bring forth 'sub-normal' and 'socially inadequate' children who were 'injurious' to society. The vagaries of the law allowed them to sterilize patients.

Even in states which had no specific sterilization law, a surgeon could legally sterilize a patient on 'therapeutic' grounds, so long as he or she had the consent of the patient, or in the case of mental incompetence or a minor, the consent of parents or guardians. This opened up the possibility for a wide abuse of medical powers along eugenic and socio-economic lines. Critics charged that doctors were free to sterilize patients whom they believed were 'unfit' to parent because they were poor. Doctors themselves admitted that they applied pressure on relatives to convince them of the benefits of remedial 'pycho-sexual' surgery. And physicians working within America's state institutions practised largely without public censure. Release from an institution may easily have been granted on condition that a patient be no threat to society, and hence be sterilized. Because a medical authority could compel patients to give consent, the distinction between voluntary and compulsory sterilization was blurred. The annual average of recorded 'voluntary' sterilizations in America was about 1,300, according to one source (Blacker 1962: 156). But estimates for these also vary enormously (Giannella 1973: 68–81). The limitations of the available statistics make it difficult for historians to assess the true impact of the American and Nazi sterilization programmes. The difference in the known number of victims of the American and German legislation does matter enormously, but the Nazi policy was harsher by a matter of degree only.

It is also important to recognize that the American and the German sterilization programmes were remarkably similar in intent given the differences in these societies. In America, the classes of persons recommended for sterilization differed by state. From its origin as a treatment for 'juvenile delinquency', compulsory sterilization became a catch-all cure for an ever widening range of social problems. As the American geneticist Madison Grant wrote in his 1916 *The Passing of the Great Race*, sterilization was a 'practical' and 'unsentimental' solution to the growing population of 'social discards' who became hopeless welfare dependants. Sterilization, he argued, should be applied not only to the criminal, diseased and insane, but also to 'types which may be called weaklings rather than defectives, and perhaps ultimately to worthless race types' (quoted in Reilly 1977: 123–4). This hard pragmatic approach was reflected in American law.

Some states preferred to sterilize mainly paupers and drunks, others drug addicts or unmarried mothers. For example, Utah authorized the sterilization of persons not capable of performing the duties of parenthood because they had an 'inborn' aversion to work and responsibility. The various compulsory laws also covered many types of criminal for whom sterilization was advised. In Oklahoma, the law permitted the sterilization of 'habitual offenders' convicted of three separate felonies. A chicken thief or armed robber could be served with a sterilization petition. However, not surprisingly, the statute excluded certain white-collar crimes such as embezzlement and tax evasion, so it was unmistakably class-based. By the end of the 1930s, the categories of persons liable for 'asexualization' numbered as many as thirty-four (Reilly 1977: 125–6; Landman 1932: 255). Being a product of puritan values, the American public health system did show a marked tendency to favour the sterilization of those guilty of 'sex perversions'. These included convictions for rape, but also a number of symptoms of 'moral degeneracy', such as suspected syphilis, 'onanism' and promiscuity. This demonstrated the extent to which sterilization legislation could be used to discriminate not only against those with certain undesirable biological traits but also against those who exhibited behaviour deemed to be dangerous. The Nazis were also concerned to eradicate forms of sexual 'deviance' as well as types of mental defect. While directives permitted the sterilization of 'moral weaklings' such as beggars, criminals and unwed mothers, most sterilizations were carried out for so-called 'hereditary feeblemindedness' and schizophrenia (Weindling 1989: 533; Burleigh and Wipperman 1991: 170). Despite some differences in their classifications of who was most injurious to the race, both the American and Nazi systems opened up new avenues for social oppression.

Categories of persons liable for sterilization were imprecise. Under the Nazi Act of 1933, like similar legislation in American states, those deemed 'feebleminded' could include simply the uneducated rather than those with proven low intelligence. And the IQ tests used to demonstrate sub-normal mental development were known to be biased and unreliable. Physical deformity as a basis for sterilization under the Nazi law also covered a wide range of ailments. While political crimes were deemed to be insufficient grounds for 'desexualization' in America, disloyalty to the Nazi regime could warrant a sterilization order for mental disorder. Both governments used flimsy medical and scientific criteria of inheritable disease as justification for programmes aimed at the elimination of social outcasts.

American legal history demonstrates that programmes contemplating major invasions of personal freedom could gather strong support despite the obvious infringements of civil liberties. The imposition of marriage prohibitions is one instance in which the state's encroachment on sexual and personal privacy is clear. In America, laws against marriages between persons of different colour were still in force in some fifteen states as recently as the 1960s. For

example, in Virginia, it was a crime for a white person to marry a
black person, but not for a black person to wed an Asian person.
These so-called 'miscegenation' statutes aimed at preserving the
purity of the 'white race' (Reilly 1977: 135; see also Haller 1963;
Ludmerer 1972). In Nazi Germany too, sexuality and reproduction
were no longer considered to be purely private matters. The dictatorship banned marriages and sexual relations between nationals of
'German or kindred blood' and Jews in 1935 (Noakes and Pridham
1984: 535–6). Mussolini's dictatorship may have eschewed a population policy based on 'negative' eugenics; but his government took
major steps towards a racial policy by prohibiting sexual congress
between Italian colonists and native subjects in East Africa in 1937,
one year before the implementation of a prohibition against marriages between members of the Italian and Jewish 'races' (Preti
1974: 190).

How these interventions happened has been associated by scholars with the ascendency of 'biomedical utopias' in the twentieth
century (Lifton 1986: 17). Utopian perspectives like those of eugenicists gained such popularity because they held out the promise that
it was scientifically possible to perfect human beings. In certain
societies, the medical and biological professions were allowed to
impose their vision of a healthy order by influencing the development of ambitious and authoritarian programmes aimed at social
engineering. The 'modern state' has also proved willing to use 'scientistic' ideologies about the inheritance of 'disease' in order to shore
up the social order. Regimes of public health policing demonstrate
to what lengths states would go to enforce the values of discipline,
work and family life within the national community. The enactment
of repressive laws also shows that eugenics in Germany and America
was not on the fringes of society but at the very centre of policy
planning. Movements there attracted the support of judges, university chairs and presidents, religious leaders, literary giants, eminent
scientists and a wide range of politicians from all parties. What
America and Germany have in common is that the impact of eugenics was great in these countries.

But we must try to avoid the temptation to label all eugenicists
as 'murderous' scientists (Müller-Hill 1988). Blaming eugenics for
the rise of hegemonic social programmes ignores the fact that the
state was very selective about which scientific and medical evidence
it used to justify policies. As early as 1912, American delegates to
the first international eugenics conference in London provided statistics to show that sterilization had failed to reduce rates of crimi-

nality and insanity in those twelve states which had compulsory laws. In the 1920s, the American Neurological Association opposed eugenic sterilization on scientific grounds. In 1937, a committee of the American Medical Association investigating the controversy reported that 'our present knowledge regarding human heredity is so limited that there appears to be very little scientific basis to justify the limitation of conception for eugenic reasons' (Paul 1973: 31).

Not all German eugenicists shared the beliefs of their colleague, Ernst Rüdin, who founded the genetic theory of psychiatry and advocated the sterilization of schizophrenics. Many were aware of the limits of their knowledge and the possibilities for the misuse of science by those with a sanitizing social agenda. Widely accepted Mendelian laws of inheritance suggested that human characteristics might be recessive and therefore might not appear in each successive generation. This realization cast doubt on the effectiveness of eugenic sterilization to wipe out unwanted disease. And compulsory sterilization came into vogue as a policy preference just as new research on DNA began to challenge existing theories about the genetic transmission of alcoholism, epilepsy and retardation (Reilly 1977: 125).

After the discoveries of Gregor Mendel were reassessed at the turn of the century, no scientist could seriously argue that 'foreign blood' could cause 'racial pollution'. Scientists knew that blood did not carry units of heredity and that inheritance was not a matter of 'blending' different characters, as Charles Darwin had thought. But 'miscegenation' laws were still enacted to prevent the 'intermingling' of races which allegedly produced new 'mixed' hybrids who were inferior to 'pure' breeds. Historians of medicine and science have tended to ascribe much of the blame for the rise of racially moti-vated reproductive policies on the expansion of the power of health care professionals in the twentieth century. But they overlook the fact that governments dictated the terms of population policies, defined the sphere of activity of doctors and scientists and implemented programmes based on clearly controvertible claims.

In America and Germany, the scientific pursuits of biomedical experts coalesced with the political objectives of interventionist governments. Both countries implemented coercive laws authorizing medical professionals to measure the worth of human life in selec-tive-breeding programmes. Both reserved the right to reproduce for those of demonstrable social value. Neither nation deemed the protection of the 'socially useless' to be more important than the interests of the state and its taxpayers. The efforts of science to attribute human traits and behaviours to inheritance provided governments with limitless possibilities for the planning of policies for racial hygiene. Seemingly 'inborn' qualities like heretical beliefs or physical characteristics like skin colour were invested with all sorts of meanings by those seeking biological solutions to social problems (Duster 1990: 1–8). But only the National Socialist state took these possibilities to the extreme.

The approach of war gave the Nazis new opportunities for the radicalization of policies for racial hygiene. In the winter of 1938, Hitler gave authorization for a top secret programme of child murder. By August 1939, the Chancellery had created a bureaucracy with a mandate to supervise the elimination of deformed and disabled infants and children up to 3 years of age. Special 'clinics' were created where doctors killed about 6,000 children and then performed autopsies on them to ascertain the causes of their defects (Weindling 1989: 545–8; Burleigh and Wipperman 1991: 142–4). An adult 'euthanasia' programme began in the summer of 1939 as the regime planned to clear hospital beds for use during the coming war. This focused on the liquidation of the mentally ill and diagnosed schizophrenics figured prominently among the estimated 70,000 to 90,000 who were transported to purpose-built medical units where they were gassed and cremated. Although it ended officially in August 1941, the 'euthanasia' programme actually continued throughout the war as the 'worthless lives' of psychiatric patients were terminated by starvation, lethal drugs and fatal injections. Old people in poor houses, sick slave workers and concentration camp inmates were also summarily murdered in a campaign that eventually resulted in the deaths of about 200,000 'anti-social' individuals (Noakes and Pridham 1988: ch. 36 and Burleigh and Wipperman 1991: 141–67). This policy of what Robert Jay Lifton called 'medical killing' has only recently received much attention, and is the subject of a long-awaited book by Michael Burleigh entitled *Death and Deliverance: Euthanasia in Germany, c.1900–45* (1994).

The Final Solution, by contrast, has long been a subject of debate. After the invasion of Poland in September 1939, expansion eastward facilitated the fulfilment of longstanding plans for the settlement of conquered lands by the Germans. According to some historians, Nazi aims focused initially on the 'Germanization' of occupied territories through the expulsion of Poles, Jews and gypsies, the 'cleansing' of subject populations by means of the elimination of all opponents, and the creation of a vast slave army of resettled foreign peoples who would serve an enlarged German state. But whether the Nazis really planned to resettle Jewish deportees on reservations on the fringes of the Reich or even expel them from Europe has remained a contentious issue. Some scholars have maintained that proposed resettlement schemes, along with the actual ghettoization of Polish Jews, were thinly disguised extermination policies which prepared the path for the Final Solution (Browning 1992: 7–27 and ch. 2).

Historians have also argued about how the so-called 'Jewish Question' resulted in the *Endlösung* (Final Solution). No agreement ever prevailed in a debate about whether the Nazis always intended to implement a policy of mass murder or whether the death camps were an *ad hoc* product of wartime conditions. At times the controversy appeared to hinge on the issue of whether the Final Solution was murder or manslaughter. Many scholars traced the origins of the Final Solution to Hitler's anti-Semitism. From as early as 1919, Hitler declared a single-minded dedication to the goal of the 'total annihilation' of the Jews. This consistency led 'intentionalist' historians to see a clear 'blueprint' for future murder in Hitler's speeches and writings. Nazi anti-Jewish policy, they argued, developed logically in a series of stages from this ideological imperative. Lucy Dawidowicz, for example, asserted that Hitler waited until the war for the right moment to realize his murderous plans (Dawidowicz 1975: 109–11). Other historians, however, were struck by the fact that so much time lapsed between the invasion of Poland in 1939 and the launch of the Final Solution in 1942.

During the course of a heated debate about which much has subsequently been written, 'functionalists' claimed that wartime policies towards the Jews evolved by improvisation and accident rather than premeditation. Hans Mommsen could find no causative connection between the fanatical anti-Semitism of *Mein Kampf* and the extermination policy conducted during the Second World War. Indeed, he argued that Nazi anti-Semitism was mere rhetoric and Hitler's *Weltanschauung* (worldview) should not be taken seriously. He depicted the Führer as a leader removed from party politics and absolved him of any blame for the Final Solution (Mommsen 1976: 197). Martin Broszat contended that the Final Solution evolved as a consequence of wartime pressures rather than careful planning. In his assessment, local party officials took the initiative to commit genocide. Broszat based this claim on the fact that historians have found no documentary evidence of a central directive from Hitler (Broszat 1979: 73–125).

However, this lack of 'proof' did not deter scholars from asserting that Hitler was directly involved in the launch of the Final Solution. Indeed, many found compelling confirmation of a 'Hitler order' in Eichmann's testimony during his trial in Jerusalem. Eichmann suggested that the decision to implement the Final Solution came directly from Hitler (Hofer 1986: 236). Based on the inability of historians to find any signed statement from Hitler, David Irving notoriously claimed that the Führer knew nothing of the extermination policy implemented by his fanatical followers (Irving 1977; Seidel 1986). But the eminent historian Raul Hilberg dismissed the rants of self-appointed apologists. He argued eloquently that although Hitler might never even have issued any written order to kill the Jews, the mandate to do so undoubtedly came from him. As was the nature of his rule, the Führer communicated his plans to top-ranking Nazis who then began the bureaucratic process of policy implementation through the hierarchical chain of command (Hilberg 1983). The quest for a written order from Hitler seems particularly ludicrous when the magnitude of the death and destruction inflicted by the extermination policy is appreciated.

Despite persistent echoes to the contrary, so-called Holocaust 'revisionism' and the 'functionalist/structuralist' controversy have run out of steam. Christopher Browning's recent 'moderate functionalist' interpretation presented a workable compromise. The Final Solution, he argued, was neither 'initiated from below by Nazi bureaucrats' nor 'implemented by explicit orders from above'. During the war, Hitler gave out 'new signals and directions' to party leaders which set in motion a series of policies culminating in the Holocaust. The 'final step' to mass murder was 'incremental' rather than a 'quantum leap' (Browning 1992: 88, 141 and 143–4). This position seems more tenable than many others. It does fail, however, to address the main argument of the functionalists, namely that the Final Solution was unplanned. Even if we consider only the problems of transport and the diversion of resources from the war effort, we are left with the unmistakable impression that not only must the initiative have come from Hitler but it must also have necessitated a huge amount of planning.

From 1938 to 1941, military conquest gave the Nazis access to millions of Jews within an empire stretching from Norway to North Africa and from the Channel Islands in the Atlantic to the outskirts of Moscow and the Crimea. The first deportations of Jews from Germany to Poland began in the autumn of 1939, and the mass transportation of Jews from Western to Eastern Europe started in the following winter. Now more than ever, the 'Jewish Question' demanded a solution. At some point, Nazi war aims decisively shifted away from mere territorial expansion towards mass murder. This watershed, Browning and others have asserted, occurred with the invasion of the Soviet Union in June 1941 (Browning 1992: 77–85).

As part of the Barbarossa attack, the Nazis systematically murdered millions of Russian Jews, Communists and prisoners of war. *Einsatzgruppen*, brigades of over 11,000 trained SS killers, followed advancing army troops and together these forces fought a war by means of mass executions (Noakes and Pridham 1988: 1086–90). Euphoria over Wehrmacht success in frenzied killing provided stimulus to other war crimes and atrocities. The Nazis mobilized a huge machinery of death and destruction in their attempt to reorganize the racial structure of Eastern Europe. Those who were unable to work or unfit to survive were eliminated. In Poland and the Soviet Union, women and children, the sick and disabled, orphans and youths were rounded up and then executed (Weindling 1989: 550). The Nazis performed compulsory abortions on women who worked in slave labour camps. And they carried out punitive sterilizations and induced abortions on local populations to prevent them from breeding (David *et al.* 1988: 100; Kudlien 1990: 240). In labour and concentration camps, Nazi doctors searched frantically for new methods to allow them to sterilize inmates as cheaply and effectively as possible. Gypsies and Jews were sterilized, painfully, unsuccessfully and often fatally as Nazis experimented on them with X-rays, uterine injections and plant extracts (Blacker 1952: 9–19). The Nazi bid for *Lebensraum*, living space for all Aryans in a vast new Germany, had accelerated into a demographic struggle against alien 'races' in which doctors used biomedical technology as a weapon of war.

Barbarossa was undoubtedly a major step towards the Final Solution. But when the 'total race war' began is a matter of some debate. Opinion differs over the actual timing of the decision to liquidate the Jews of Europe. Some scholars believe an order from the Führer came as early as March 1941, and others contend that it did so sometime either in the summer or the autumn of that year (Marrus 1988: 32–4; Breitman 1991: 20–6). Whatever the truth may be, extensive planning for genocide undoubtedly occurred. The terrifying efficiency of the administrative system for extermination which the Nazis quickly created also debunks the persistent myth that this was a weak dictatorship. The *Endlösung* apparently came about with little internal party friction and with much complicity among bureaucrats. From the autumn of 1941, Nazi scouts sought out appropriate sites for the construction of death camps. Perpetrators of the 'euthanasia' programme were transferred to the East, where they helped build the gas chambers for genocide. The machinery of mass murder was already in place by December 1941 when the first camps were opened in Poland (Noakes and Pridham 1988: ch. 39). During the final stages of what unquestionably became 'a war against the Jews', the Nazis intensified their search for the most cost-effective and scientific methods for the murder of millions.

The death camp was a peculiarly Nazi invention, a terrible reminder that during the Third Reich medicine, science and the state colluded in the implementation of a population and race policy whose ultimate aim was genocide. It also testified to the profound brutalization of conscience effected by a Nazi value system which 'normalized' and 'routinized' the torture and murder of people considered to be less than human. After initial dissatisfaction with the progress of the killing, the Nazis perfected their extermination techniques by pushing existing technology to the limits and enlisting the services of industrialists, bureaucrats, chemists, architects and other professionals. As new camps were built, specialists made improvements in the design of buildings and in the methods of murder. Experts devised more effective poisons, mechanized the assembly line for entry and selection and rationalized the process of gassing and burning. At their model camp at Auschwitz-Birkenau, the Nazis proudly achieved near perfection in meeting 'productivity' targets as the gas chamber there could accommodate as many as 2,000 victims at a time. Under the leadership of the SS, camp scientists and doctors enjoyed free reign to pursue their clinical research. They took advantage of this unprecedented opportunity by performing fatal medical experiments on the 'Jewish vermin' who, they reasoned, were destined to die anyway (Koonz 1987: ch. 11). To the end of the Nazi race war, medicine and science proved to be willing accomplices of the genocidal state.

4   Conclusion

The politics of race and population in the twentieth century

That mass murder was an instrument of a Nazi Utopia demonstrates beyond any doubt that the Third Reich's racialized population policy was indeed unique. The magnitude of the death and destruction brought about by National Socialism cannot be ignored, even though the core thinking behind Nazism's programme of race hygiene invites obvious comparisons with the ideas behind policies implemented in other countries. The logic of Nazi ideology on race and population centred around the familiar notion of 'selective breeding', a concept which also found many followers in other nations, but one which was relentlessly taken to the extreme of 'exterminism' only by Nazism. In the pursuit of a vision of a perfected Aryan race enjoying mastery over a racially cleansed Europe, the Nazi state persecuted its own citizens, infants, women, the aged, the handicapped, ethnic and religious minorities and many others by means of sterilization, then 'euthanasia', and ultimately, genocide. The goal of a hierarchical New Racial Order was the driving force and *raison d'être* of Nazism. Quite simply, the totality of measures to perfect the race which culminated in the Final Solution differentiates German population policy from that of any other nation, even from that of the other fascist dictatorship in Italy.

The primacy of race in Nazi population policy and ideology distinguishes Germany from other countries. Recognition of the importance of racial imperatives to all Nazi initiatives in the spheres of foreign and domestic policies, however, does not render comparisons to other countries useless. Recently, Michael Burleigh and Wolfgang Wipperman published an important book, the first systematic and comprehensive study of all aspects of the Nazi 'racial-ideological programme'. These scholars argue persuasively that the Nazis were committed to a vision of an 'ideal future world, without "lesser races", without the sick, and without those who they decreed had no

place in the "national community" '. Because of the Third Reich's
fanatical pursuit of its racial-ideological objectives, the various
elements of Nazi race and population policy should be seen as an
'indivisible whole'. Burleigh and Wipperman advance our understanding of Nazism by demonstrating that the instruments of totalitarian rule in Germany were used to realize a 'barbarous utopia'.
None the less, these historians revive a defunct debate about fascism
and modernization in order to resuscitate old arguments that Germany followed a 'separate road of historical development'. The
authors repeatedly insist on observance of the 'specific and singular
character of the Third Reich'. They contend that the Nazi dictatorship was 'a regime without precedent or parallel' (Burleigh and
Wipperman 1991: 4, 304 and 306).

To rehearse past discussions about the pros and cons of
approaches which seek to generalize about history is beyond the
scope of this book. The outmoded modernization debates of the
1960s did have serious faults in that some of the key contributors
imposed theories and 'models' emerging out of the social, economic
and political sciences on complex historical phenomena. History was
often made to 'fit' the elaborate theories by over-simplification and
distortion of evidence. Burleigh and Wipperman are right to insist
on the specificity of history. However, interpretations which focus
too narrowly on the developments within single nations are no less
limited in usefulness than those which range their vision too widely.
Scholars must attempt to explore genuinely comparable trends in
different countries or they are at risk of saying nothing meaningful
at all.

This book has attempted to argue that the path revisionism should
take in the future is to reassess fascism by comparing it systematically and historically to conventional political systems, like liberal
parliamentary democracies, and other exceptional states, such as
Communist dictatorships. For far too long scholars have asked themselves 'what is fascism?' and have tried to answer this question by
comparing like with like. So seemingly 'fascist' movements and
regimes have been analysed at length, while similarities between
outwardly disparate political forms have been ignored to the detriment of our understanding of the linkages and parallels between
fascist, democratic and Communist countries. We can only identify
what is uniquely 'fascist' about the German and Italian dictatorships
by comparing these to other kinds of governments.

Limiting discussion to the specific topic of this book, we realize
when we disregard the tenets of an orthodoxy which believes in the

exceptionalism of fascism that many of the tenets of the Nazi brand of race hygiene only seem unique if one is ignorant of the aims of eugenics in other countries. Other nations besides Germany contributed to the history of ideas about compulsory abortions, 'selective breeding', 'racial cleansing', 'euthanasia', extermination and so on. While the Third Reich may or may not have been a distinct political system, depending on whether one adheres to the 'totalitarian' model, and on whether one's perspective is focused on Europe, the world, all dictatorships, or only 'fascist' ones, it seems pointless to blind oneself purposefully to the reality that in many respects Germany was not so exceptional after all. There were profound parallels in the historical development of modern nations which gave rise to shared concerns about degeneration and depopulation and a common faith in population planning as the best way forward for governments. The brutal ferocity and efficiency with which the Nazi state pursued its racialized ideological imperatives seems to me to be a chilling reminder that the power of this dictatorship was indeed unequalled in Western Europe in the interwar period. But the ideas which informed the Third Reich's racial programmes were prevalent in other countries too.

Scholars are still reluctant to demystify the social agendas set by fascist regimes by comparing them to those of conventional political systems. The prevalence of expressions of profound concern over a shrinking and differential birthrate should not be overlooked by those who limit their perspective to the history of single nations. The belief that the working-class residuum of the population, who reputedly gave birth to 'born' criminals, the insane, paupers and prostitutes, should not propagate imprudently found followers in America, Britain and Germany. In these countries, planners were motivated by the élitist aims that only citizens of the 'right breed' should increase their fertility. They came to uphold the view that biological degeneration could be averted solely by means of regulated and restricted population growth. In Britain, population theorists blamed the 'hereditarily unfit' members of the lower orders for the nation's imperial and industrial decline. In America and Germany, Social Darwinist prejudices about the proletariat's impaired inheritance found expression in reform proposals to safeguard the race. Although there were important differences in the approach taken and the policies pursued in these countries, there were also significant similarities which scholars should not ignore.

But this is hardly surprising. As this book has attempted to show, comparative study of demographic debates can provide important insight into the many varieties and common features of nationalism at a moment of crisis and reflection. Perceptions of progress changed dramatically at the end of the nineteenth century as precipitous birthrate decline gave contemporaries reason to believe that evolution could be regressive as well as progressive. Prevalent throughout modern culture and politics, fear of degeneration afflicted many different countries. New nationalisms based on biological theories about society emerged as a consequence of widespread anxiety over the menace of depopulation. But out of this initial panic arose a new vision of the domain and scope of politics as experts called upon governments to regulate sex and reproduction in the nation's interest. Society became a laboratory and the body a battleground for would-be planners urging politicians to intervene directly in the evolutionary process. As a cultural value, respect for personal reproductive and sexual freedoms was superseded by commitment to the idea that individual rights were secondary to those of the collectivity. Many believed that the national interest lay in altering fertility by means of aggressive and authoritarian interventions in private life. This widespread notion that the state should control reproduction lay at the very foundation of population policies in both dictatorships and democracies. Although Nazism shaped existing ideas into its own distinct vision of a New Racial Order, one which defined selectionism and exterminism as a means to Utopia, the Third Reich's ideology and policies were part of this larger historical process.

This brings us to the conclusion that many of the features which scholars commonly define as 'fascist' were not the exclusive preserve of the Italian and German dictatorships. Moreover, the Italian and German varieties of fascism diverged substantially in their aims. Mussolini's frantic bid to boost the birthrate, for example, shared more in common with the policies introduced by successive Third Republic governments than it did with Nazi race hygiene. French measures to protect the race focused more on the endowment of fatherhood through special privileges, and Italian reforms, had they been implemented in their entirety, would have brought substantial benefits to mothers. Nevertheless, they were both resolutely pronatalist in their aims. That the two 'core' countries which went fascist in interwar Europe should have had such different racial objectives bears directly on our understanding of what scholars call 'generic' fascism.

Dissimilarity between Italy and Germany debunks the persistent myth that there was something peculiarly 'fascist' about the adoption of an aggressive and authoritarian population policy. The pronatalist campaign of Mussolini brought fascist Italy more in line with Catholic nations like France than it did with Protestant ones like Germany. The goal of fertility increase motivated both a parliamentary democracy in Third Republic France and a fascist dictatorship in Italy to enact protective legislation affecting women, men and the family. In both these countries, 'positive' measures to stimulate the birthrate formed the basis of major social reforms. Fascist Italy's demographic campaign shared the goals, if not all of the means, of the pronatalist policies pursued by Third Republic governments. Because the Pope's 1930 encyclical, *Casti Connubi*, condemned the inhibition of procreation through use of any 'artificial' form of birth control as a crime against God and nature, even those eugenicists who condoned sterilization on eugenic grounds could not bring themselves to advocate its adoption publicly.

The encyclical also dealt specifically with the issue of eugenic sterilization, both so-called 'voluntary' and explicitly compulsory, and defined this as a violation of the integrity and sanctity of the body which was both unlawful and immoral according to Church doctrine. Like their American, English and German colleagues, eugenicists in France and Italy did debate about whether the social application of 'negative' measures to regulate fertility could really effect biological improvements in future generations. They discussed the feasibility of marital prohibitions for the hereditarily unfit, the institutionalization of the biologically unsound and the sterilization of the hopelessly degenerate. Scientists and doctors coolly evaluated whether poisoning testicles and ovaries by means of radiation and iodine was a more effective preventive measure for 'desexualization' than removing reproductive organs by surgery.

But in France and Italy, eugenicists shied away from endorsing radical methods of protecting racial patrimony from pollution because they recognized the social primacy of the Church. They did not wish to jeopardize their chances of influencing prospective population policies by alienating conservative and Catholic opinion. And financial considerations also posed an obstacle to the formulation of strategies for population planning requiring massive taxation and spending. Although sterilization was widely acknowledged to be a cheaper way of promoting public health than state-funded social welfare, its organization into a mass programme would still require a large amount of resources. Italian eugenic lobbyists, in particular, simply believed that the state, in both its liberal and fascist forms, was far too poor and weak to fund and implement any reform necessitating mass screening for disease and defect. Rejection of a Nazi-style policy for race hygiene in confessional nations rested not on moral objections so much as on practical considerations (Quine 1990: 18–21; Schneider 1990: 71–2, 89 and 109).

Only after military defeat and the collapse of the Third Republic in 1940 did racist, anti-Semitic and anti-immigrant hatreds begin to influence French population policy. While few French populationists supported the more extreme aspects of Nazi race hygiene, many endorsed less radical proposals for sound breeding. Influenced by moderately 'negative' eugenics, the Vichy government launched a policy of preventive racial health protection. A premarital examination act of 1942 forced couples to pass tests for transmittable diseases before marriage. Although it did not prohibit people with a diagnosed 'inferior' inheritance from marrying, the legislation was the first of its kind in France (Schneider 1990: 256 and 268–71). Although rather mild compared to some of the more hideous elements of the Nazi programme of 'negative' eugenics, the idea of premarital screening found little favour in a fascist regime which could not countenance the introduction of such a controversial measure. Despite the fact that some Italian eugenicists lobbied on behalf of health testing before marriage, Mussolini's regime resisted calls to implement even the most benign of antinatalist reforms (Quine forthcoming: pt. 1).

Historians have been somewhat slow to realize that eugenics took on many different forms and that German race hygiene was merely one offshoot of an international movement with many national variations. 'Eugenics' is still so associated with 'Nazism' in our minds that we are blind to the reality that the reformist ideas which grew out of it had a broad geographic but highly differentiated impact. Although they took on various forms, nationalist initiatives to repopulate and regenerate society were not exclusive to Nazi Germany. Scholars have also argued wrongly that Italian eugenicists did not seriously contemplate the benefits which programmes for mass compulsory sterilization might have brought to a noble, but ageing and degenerate race (Weindling 1987: 22). In Catholic countries like France, Italy and Spain, milder varieties of eugenics prevailed in spite of the fact that practitioners were no less attracted to the utopian idea of the perfectibility of humankind than were Nazi planners. Unlike 'positive' eugenics, which promised to introduce only gradual improvements in the biological make-up of the race, sterilization and other 'negative' measures seemed to hold out the possibility that evolutionary selection could be accelerated and favourable adaptations could be forced to emerge within the space of one or two generations. Had Italian and French eugenic science and medicine enjoyed the same sort of freedom from constraints that they did in Nazi Germany, then the unthinkable might very well have happened in these countries too. Nazism unleashed a 'totalitarian' bio-power over the body which doctors and scientists in other nations also craved. And this bears directly upon the insights provided by a spate of research engendered by the writings of Michel Foucault.

Foucault's enduring influence has led to the publication of a slew of books which have argued that ideas about progress, evolution and heredity were used by psychiatrists and other medical élites to advance their professions, further scientific research, expand career opportunities, gain control of public health administration and ultimately to assert their power over society. The works of J. Edward Chamberlin, Sander L. Gilman and Daniel Pick explored how the idea of degeneration permeated culture in the nineteenth century, exercised 'dominion' over the collective imagination and reflected deep fears of national decline and social decay (Chamberlin and Gilman 1985: viii; Pick 1989). Elaine Showalter, Lynda Nead, Cynthia Eagle Russett and many others have shown how changing perceptions about women's inferiority, deviance and transgression in the nineteenth century influenced the reforms and arrangements which institutionalized female oppression in Victorian Britain (Showalter 1987; Nead 1988; Eagle Russett 1989).

The importance of these topics has now been well established by more than a decade of intense research into social constructions of sexuality, race, gender, disease, disorder and Utopia. The thesis that men of science and medicine succeeded in wielding a total biomedical 'hegemony' and ruled over our bodies has become familiar to anyone interested in 'new' history. What is sometimes lost sight of in accounts, however, is the specific historical context in which ideas were translated into concrete policies affecting people. In the case of population policy, for example, it would be wrong to ignore that it took the most 'totalitarian' of all interwar dictatorships to give decidedly 'dangerous' and 'murderous' ideas shape and meaning. How science and medicine interacted not just with the broad social values of bourgeois élites but also with the precise political agendas of interventionist governments must be examined more systematically if we are to understand fully the process by which nineteenth-century population debates became twentieth-century population policies.

The distinctive features of the Nazi programme of race hygiene should not deter us from recognizing that many nations, some of which were proud democracies like America, also implemented aggressive and activist policies aimed at biological engineering and social regimentation. State interventionism in the private spheres of sexuality, behaviour and reproduction was not a unique form of fascist governance. Nor were authoritarian attempts to regulate fertility exclusive to dictatorships. New research has rightly placed the problem of the rise of modern population policies after 1870 within the broader context of how different societies adapted to the pressures exerted by the complex and contradictory processes of 'modernization'. Industrialization, imperialism, mass society, class conflict and urbanization posed unprecedented challenges for inspired governments and created new opportunities for socio-biological control.

The mode of transition to modernity may have differed in each individual country, but the challenges posed were shared by many nations. In the twentieth century, states have gone well beyond the mere enactment of social security laws covering sickness, old age, unemployment and labour conditions. They have sought to effect dramatic socio-biological change in populations through a variety of conspicuously coercive and apparently progressive reforms. Demographic anxiety in both dictatorships and democracies provided the emotional and ideological stimulus for the population policies which were central to the modern welfare state.

Ultimately, wider recognition that populationist concerns lie at the centre of much modern social policy will foster a revision of views about the nature of the 'welfare state'. Much controversy remains about the actual aims and achievements of increasing state regulation and centralization of social provision for families, women, children, men and workers. An older generation of scholars chose to depict the rise of the health, welfare and education policies associated with the modern state as a consequence of the transformation of uncaring and 'traditional' societies into humane and 'civilized' nations. Historians of Britain, in particular, have been inclined to describe British welfare-state building from the nineteenth century as a process linked to gradual democratization and the advance of progress engendered by benevolent governments and reform-minded parliaments (Bruce 1972: Introduction; and see Marshall 1963; de Swaan 1988: Introduction; Baldwin 1990: 8, ch. 1

and 232–47). By contrast, the rather comprehensive but notorious protective legislation introduced by Bismarck, and by other unpalatable political leaders on the Continent, such as Mussolini, appears to be far less progressive in motivation. Indeed, welfare in nations outside of Britain, and a few other exemplary nations like Sweden, is seen by some scholars as a cheap bid to buy off the working class, a counter-revolutionary, manipulative and downright deplorable strategy used by repressive regimes seeking to take the wind out of organized socialism and the labour movement. The time has come for scholars to bury the old myth that the classic Welfare State in Britain was some kind of historical aberration, an expression of the British sense of decency, fairness and justice. Many of the concerns about the quality and quantity of population which stimulated interest in welfare reform in the twentieth century were shared by liberal, fascist and socialist politicians. Political self-interest on the part of different governments, rather than enlightened altruism, led to the development of state-run systems of welfare.

The failure of the racialized forms of 'biological politics' implemented by interwar governments has not led to the abandonment of attempts to influence fertility. The attractions of population policies for nations have always been the promise they held that social problems could be solved through direct and immediate governmental action. The decades after 1945 have seen the reappearance of demographic debates in different countries, many of them outside the industrialized world. Apparent 'over-population' in the so-called Third World has led to the imposition of programmes for compulsory planned parenthood on many different peoples. Potential military and industrial prowess is still tied to the issue of the size of the population in public opinion and policy. Developing nations have felt the need to limit demographic growth in order to improve general living standards and enter the family of advanced economies.

Swings and shifts in the birthrate still affect aspirations and anxieties about national grandeur and decline in Europe as well. With continued birthrate decline throughout much of the postwar period, pronatalism has proved to be an enduring feature of politics. Recurring panics over the threat of 'depopulation' and periodic outcries about the imminent demise of the family have frequently become a pivot of nationalist rhetoric designed to rally the general public at moments of crisis. At the end of the twentieth century, the question of reproductive freedoms and choices has yet to be solved. Abortion remains very much on the political agenda, as do matters relating to alternative sexuality and lifestyle. Programmes affecting the 'quality' of the population have also reappeared in different guises during the postwar years.

Discrimination against racial and ethnic minorities within the population has not ceased to be a major source of conflict and debate. Government authorities have repeatedly stirred up anger against various 'social problem groups' to mobilize support for punitive and restrictive policies aimed at reducing public spending on the poor. While allegedly rising rates of alcohol abuse gave interwar parliaments inspiration for moral crusades, politicians now launch a 'war on drugs' when they want to appear to be providing strong leadership and inspired governance. Much maligned by political leaders and the press, lone mothers still come under attack for being promiscuous 'recidivists' who produce too many bastard babies who grow up to be 'juvenile delinquents' and 'welfare-dependants'. The single-parent family is perceived as a major threat to the social order, as are forms of family formation, such as homosexual coupling, which deviate from the prevailing prescriptive ideal.

Postwar demographic change has also had an enormous impact on the development of social policy in new directions. Because of greater affluence and technological advance in medicine, life spans have increased in the West and this has provoked worry over an ageing population. The rise in the number of people surviving well beyond retirement age has strained the fragile foundations of welfare states already threatened by the end of a prolonged postwar period of rising productivity and full employment in the mid-1970s. Repeated recession in the 1980s caused economic resources to shrink and governments to make hard decisions about who is most 'worthy' of publicly-funded assistance. As in the 1930s, collectivist principles of universal access to state welfare and social justice for all have come under attack by those who seek to devolve public responsibility for the care of citizens back on to the individual, charity and the family. A revival of archaic poor law programmes for self-help and voluntarism has accompanied the extension of means-testing to restrict mass eligibility to benefits.

And the neo-fascist Right throughout Europe has resuscitated old arguments about women's place and the menace of immigration. For decades after the Second World War, it seemed that racist and sexist ideological imperatives had disappeared permanently from the rhetoric which surrounded the Welfare State. The language of welfare and population changed dramatically after 1945 when policymakers sanitized it of terms associated with eugenics and fascism.

But now, the mobilization of discontent among the youth of Europe by the militant and nationalist Right incites hatred towards racial, ethnic and religious minorities and inspires fear about the imagined purity and supremacy of race. Demands for a closure of national borders to 'foreigners', the withdrawal of social rights from immigrants and the removal of women from the workforce reflect a profound cultural crisis no less severe than that which anticipated by decades the rise of fascism in the 1920s. Right-wing ideologues who now call themselves 'post-fascists' are even bandying about the rather unoriginal notions that the family and motherhood must be protected from the threatening and alien forces within a New Europe whose future remains uncertain. The politics of race has returned, while the politics of population still continues to rule over our lives and our bodies.

Bibliography

The bibliography is arranged by chapter heading and lists all works which have been cited in the text. If a work has been cited in more than one chapter, it appears only once in the bibliography. A separate section at the end provides reference to other sources which might be of interest to the reader.

INTRODUCTION: FEARS OF 'OVER-POPULATION' AND 'DEPOPULATION' IN THE NINETEENTH CENTURY

Bennett, J. H., *Natural Selection, Heredity, and Eugenics*, New York and Oxford 1983.

Bowler, P., 'Malthus, Darwin and the Concept of Struggle', *Journal of the History of Ideas*, 37 (1976), 631–50.

D'Arcy, F., 'The Malthusian League and the Resistance to Birth Control Propaganda in Late Victorian Britain', *Population Studies*, 31 (1977), 429–48.

Fairchilds, C., 'Female Sexual Attitudes and the Rise of Illegitimacy: A Case Study', *Journal of Interdisciplinary History*, VIII (1978), 627–69.

Haller, M. H., *Eugenics: Hereditarian Attitudes in American Thought*, New Brunswick, New Jersey 1963.

Halliday, R. J., 'Social Darwinism: A Definition', *Victorian Studies*, 14 (1971), 389–406.

Kevles, D. J., *In the Name of Eugenics: Genetics and the Uses of Human Heredity*, Middlesex 1985.

Knight, P., 'Women and Abortion in Victorian and Edwardian England', *History Workshop Journal*, 4 (1977), 57–82.

McLaren, A., *Birth Control in Nineteenth-century England*, London 1978.

—— *Reproductive Rituals: the Perception of Fertility in England from the Sixteenth to the Nineteenth Century*, London and New York 1984.

—— *Sexuality and Social Order: the Debate Over the Fertility of Women and Workers in France, 1770–1920*, New York and London 1983.

Malthus, T. R., *An Essay on the Principle of Population*, London 1982. Introduction by T. H. Hollingsworth.

Nisot, M. T., *La question eugénique dans les divers pays*, vol. II, Brussels 1929.

Noonan, Jr., J. T., *Contraception: A History of its Treatment by the Catholic Theologians and Canonists*, Cambridge, Massachusetts 1966.

Problems in Eugenics: First International Eugenics Conference, 1912, Held at the University of London, July 24–30, 1912, in C. Rosenberg, ed., *The History of Hereditarian Thought*, New York and London 1984.

Problems in Eugenics: Papers Communicated to the First International Eugenics Conference Held at the University of London, July 24–30, 1912, vols I and II, London 1912 and 1913.

Quine, M. S., 'From Malthus to Mussolini: The Italian Eugenics Movement and Fascist Population Policy, 1890–1938', PhD thesis, University of London, 1990.

Rose, P., *Parallel Lives: Five Victorian Marriages*, New York 1984.

Shorter, E., 'Illegitimacy, Sexual Revolution and Social Change in Modern Europe', *Journal of Interdisciplinary History*, II (1971), 237–72.

—— *The Making of the Modern Family*, New York and London 1976.

Tilly, L. A., Scott, J. W. and Cohen, M., 'Women's Work and European Fertility Patterns', *Journal of Interdisciplinary History*, VI (1976), 447–77.

Tilly, L. A. and Scott, J. W., *Women, Work, and Family*, New York 1978.

Young, R. M., 'Malthus and the Evolutionists: The Common Context of Biological and Social Theory', *Past and Present*, 43 (1969), 109–41.

1 FROM MALTHUS TO MUSSOLINI: FASCIST ITALY'S 'BATTLE FOR BIRTHS'

Bacci, M. L., *Donna, Fecondità e Figli: Due Secoli di Storia Demografica Italiana*, Bologna 1980.

Bacci, M. L. and Breschi, M., 'Italian Fertility: An Historical Account', *Journal of Family History*, 15 (1990), 385–408.

Barbagli, M., *Sotto lo Stesso Tetto*, Bologna 1984.

Bernardini, G., 'The Origins and Development of Racial Anti-Semitism in Fascist Italy', *Journal of Modern History*, 49 (1977), 431–53.

Brookes, B., 'Women and Reproduction, c. 1860–1919', in J. Lewis, ed., *Labour and Love: Women's Experience of Home and Family, 1840–1940*, Oxford 1986, 149–75.

Bull, A. and Corner, P., *From Peasant to Entrepreneur: The Survival of the Family Economy in Italy*, Providence, RI and Oxford, 1993.

Cannistraro, P. V., 'Mussolini's Cultural Revolution: Fascist or Nationalist?', *Journal of Contemporary History*, 7 (1972), 115–39.

Cardoza, A. L., 'Agrarians and Industrialists: the Evolution of an Alliance in the Po Delta, 1896–1920', in J. A. Davis, ed., *Gramsci and Italy's Passive Revolution*, London 1979.

—— *Agrarian Elites and Italian Fascism: The Province of Bologna, 1901–1926*, Princeton, New Jersey 1982.

Cenna, G., 'L'Idea Razzista nel Pensiero di Guiseppe Sergi', *Razza e Civiltà*, 1 (1940), 44–6.

Cohen, J., 'Fascism and Agriculture in Italy: Policies and Consequences', *Economic History Review*, XXXII (1979), 70–87.

Corner, P., 'Fascist Agrarian Policy and the Italian Economy in the Inter-

142 *Bibliography*

war Years', in J. A. Davis, ed., *Gramsci and Italy's Passive Revolution*, London 1979, 239–74.

—— 'Women and Fascism: Changing Family Roles in the Transition from an Agricultural to an Industrial Society', *European History Quarterly*, 23 (1993), 51–68.

De Grazia, V., *How Fascism Ruled Women: Italy, 1922–1945*, Berkeley, California 1992.

De Longis, R., 'In Difesa della Donna e della Razza', *Nuova dwf: donna, woman, femme*, 21 (1982), 149–77.

Del Panta, L., 'Italy', in W. R. Lee, ed., *European Demography and Economic Growth*, London 1979, 196–218.

Delzell, C. F., ed., *Mediterranean Fascism, 1919–45*, New York 1971.

Federico, G. and Toniolo, G., 'Italy', in R. Sylla and G. Toniolo, eds, *Patterns of European Industrialization: The Nineteenth Century*, London and New York 1992, 197–217.

Gentile, E., 'Fascism as Political Religion', *Journal of Contemporary History*, 25 (1990), 229–51.

Glass, D. V., *Population Policies and Movements in Europe*, reprint of the 1940 edition, London 1967.

Glass, D. V. and Blacker, C. P., *Population and Fertility*, London 1939.

Gregor, A. J., *Interpretations of Fascism*, Morristown, New Jersey 1974.

Griffin, R., *The Nature of Fascism*, London 1991.

Hogan, D. and Kertzer, D., 'The Social Bases of Declining Infant Mortality: Lessons from a Nineteenth-Century Italian Town', *European Journal of Population*, 2 (1986), 361–85.

Kertzer, D. I., *Family Life in Central Italy, 1880–1910: Sharecropping, Wage Labor and Coresidence*, New Brunswick, New Jersey 1984.

Kertzer, D. I. and Hogan, D. P., *Family, Political Economy, and Demographic Change: The Transformation of Life in Casalecchio, Italy, 1861–1921*, Madison, Wisconsin 1989.

Lanaro, S., *Nazione e Lavoro: Saggio sulla Cultura Borghese in Italia, 1870–1925*, Venice 1979.

Manoukian, A., 'La Famiglia dei Contadini', in P. Melograni, ed., *La Famiglia Italiana dall'Ottocento a Oggi*, Rome-Bari 1988, 3–61.

Mason, T., 'Women in Germany, 1925–1940', parts I and II, *History Workshop Journal*, 1 and 2 (1976), 74–113 and 5–31.

Merkl, P. H., 'Comparing Fascist Movements', in S. U. Larsen, B. Hagtvet, J. P. Myklebust, eds, *Who Were the Fascists?: Social Roots of European Fascism*, Bergen and Oslo 1980, 752–83.

Mosse, G. L., *The Nationalization of the Masses: Political Symbolism and Mass Movements in Germany from the Napoleonic Wars Through the Third Reich*, New York 1975.

Musso, S., 'La Famiglia Operaia', in P. Melograni, ed., *La Famiglia Italiana dall'Ottocento a Oggi*, Rome-Bari 1988, 61–106.

Noether, E., 'Italian Women and Fascism', *Italian Quarterly*, XXIII (1982), 69–80.

Ogden, P. E. and Huss, M. M., 'Demography and Pronatalism in France in the Nineteenth and Twentieth Centuries', *Journal of Historical Geography*, 8 (1982), 283–98.

Sarti, R., 'Mussolini and the Industrial Leadership in the Battle for the Lira, 1925–1927', *Past and Present*, 47 (1970), 97–112.

Serpieri, A., *La Guerra e le Classi Rurali Italiane*, Bari 1930.

—— *Studi sui Contratti Agrari*, Bologna 1920.

Turner, Jr., H. A., 'Fascism and Modernization', in H. A. Turner, Jr. ed., *Reappraisals of Fascism*, New York 1975.

Wanrooij, B. P. F., *Storia del Pudore: La Questione Sessuale in Italia, 1860–1940*, Venice 1990.

Weber, E., *Varieties of Fascism: Doctrines of Revolution in the Twentieth Century*, Princeton, New Jersey 1964.

Welk, W. G., *Fascist Economic Policy: An Analysis of Italy's Economic Experiment*, Cambridge, Massachusetts 1938.

—— *Population and History*, New York 1969.

Wrigley, E. A., *Industrial Growth and Population Change*, Cambridge, England 1961.

2 FATHERS OF THE NATION: FRENCH PRONATALISM DURING THE THIRD REPUBLIC

Beale, O. C., *Racial Decay: A Compilation of Evidence from World Sources*, Sidney, Australia 1911.

Bernard, L., *La défense de la santé publique pendant la guerre*, Paris 1929.

Bertillon, J., *La dépopulation de la France: ses conséquences – ses causes – mesures a prendre pour la combattre*, Paris 1911.

Brooke, M. Z., *Le Play: Engineer and Social Scientist*, London 1970.

Cova, A., 'French Feminism and Maternity: Theories and Policies, 1890–1945', in G. Bock and P. Thane, eds, *Maternity and Gender Policies: Women and the Rise of the European Welfare States, 1880s–1950s*, London and New York 1991, 119–37.

Del Campo, S., 'Spain', in B. Berelson, ed., *Population Policy in Developed Countries*, New York 1974, 489–544.

Gallagher, T., 'The Mystery Train: Portugal's Military Dictatorship, 1926–32', *European Studies Review*, 11 (1981), 325–53.

Griffiths, R., *Marshal Pétain*, London 1970.

Hilden, P., *Working Women and Socialist Politics in France, 1880–1914*, Oxford 1986.

Hunter, J. C., 'The Problem of the French Birthrate on the Eve of World War I', *French Historical Studies*, II (1962), 490–503.

Huss, M. M., 'Pronatalism in the Interwar Period in France', *Journal of Contemporary History*, 25 (1990), 39–68.

Le Play, M. F., *L'organisation de la famille*, Paris 1871.

Leys Stepan, N., 'Eugenics in Brazil, 1917–1940', in M. B. Adams, ed., *The Wellborn Science: Eugenics in Germany, France, Brazil, and Russia*, New York and Oxford 1990, 110–52.

McLaren, A., 'Abortion in France: Women and the Regulation of Family Size, 1800–1914', *French Historical Studies*, X (1978), 461–85.

—— 'Sex and Socialism: The Opposition of the French Left to Birth Control in the Nineteenth Century', *Journal of the History of Ideas*, XXXVI (1976), 475–92.

March, L., 'The Consequences of War and the Birth Rate in France', in *Genetics and the Family*, vol. I, *Scientific Papers of the Second International Congress on Eugenics Held at the American Museum of Natural History, New York, September 22–28, 1921*, Baltimore, Maryland 1921, 243–65.

Nash, M., 'Pronatalism and Motherhood in Franco's Spain', in G. Bock and P. Thane, eds, *Maternity and Gender Policies: Women and the Rise of the European Welfare States, 1880s–1950s*, London and New York 1991, 160–77.

Offen, K., 'Body Politics: Women, Work and the Politics of Motherhood in France, 1920–1950', in G. Bock and P. Thane, eds, *Maternity and Gender Policies: Women and the Rise of European Welfare States, 1880s–1950s*, London and New York 1991, 138–59.

Paxton, R., *Vichy France: Old Guard and New Order*, New York 1972.

Prost, A., 'Catholic Conservatives, Population, and the Family in Twentieth-Century France', in M. S. Teitelbaum and J. M. Winter, eds, *Population and Resources in Western Intellectual Traditions*, Cambridge and New York 1989, 147–64.

Quine, M. S., *The Fascist Social Revolution: The Welfare State in Italy, 1922–1945*, forthcoming, Oxford 1996.

Reynolds, S., 'Who Wanted the Crèches?: Working Mothers and the Birth-Rate in France, 1900–1950', *Continuity and Change*, 5 (1990), 173–97.

Rollet, H., *Sur le chantier social: l'action social des catholiques en France, 1870–1940*, Lyon 1955.

Schmitter, P. C., 'The Social Origins, Economic Bases and Political Imperatives of Authoritarian Rule in Portugal', in S. U. Larsen, B. Hagtvet, and J. P. Myklebust, eds, *Who Were the Fascists: Social Roots of European Fascism*, Bergen and Oslo 1980, 435–66.

Schneider, W., 'Toward the Improvement of the Human Race: The History of Eugenics in France', *The Journal of Modern History*, 54 (1982), 268–91.

—— *Quality and Quantity: The Quest For Biological Regeneration in Twentieth-Century France*, Cambridge, England 1990.

Spengler, J. J., *France Faces Depopulation*, Durham, North Carolina 1938.

Talmy, R., *Histoire du movement familial en France, 1896–1939*, 2 vols, Paris 1962.

Tomlinson, R., 'The "Disappearance" of France, 1896–1940: French Politics and the Birth Rate', *The Historical Journal*, 28 (1985), 405–15.

—— 'The Politics of Dénatalité during the French Third Republic, 1890–1940', PhD thesis, University of Cambridge, 1983.

Toulemon, A., *Le suffrage familial: ou suffrage universel intégral, le vote des femmes*, Paris 1933.

Vibart, H. H. R., *Family Allowances in Practice: An Examination of the Development of the Family Wage System and of the Compensation Fund Principally in Belgium, France, Germany and Holland*, London 1926.

Winter, J. M., 'Socialism, Social Democracy, and Population Questions in Western Europe, 1870–1950', in M. S. Teitelbaum and J. M. Winter, eds., *Population and Resources in Western Intellectual Traditions*, Cambridge and New York 1988, 122–46.

Zeldin, T., *France, 1848–1945*, vol. II, *Intellect, Taste and Anxiety*, Oxford 1977.

3 NAZI POPULATION POLICY: PRONATALISM AND ANTINATALISM DURING THE THIRD REICH

Adams, M. B., ed., *The Wellborn Science: Eugenics in Germany, France, Brazil, and Russia*, New York and Oxford 1990, 3–7.

Arendt, H., *The Origins of Totalitarianism*, Cleveland and New York 1962.

Ayçoberry, P., *The Nazi Question: An Essay on the Interpretations of National Socialism (1922–1975)*, New York 1981.

Blackbourn, D. and Eley, D., *The Peculiarities of German History: Bourgeois Society and Politics in Nineteenth-Century Germany*, Oxford 1984.

Blacker, C. P., ' "Eugenic" Experiments Conducted by the Nazis on Human Subjects', *The Eugenics Review*, 44 (1952), 9–19.

—— 'Voluntary Sterilization: Transitions Throughout the World', *The Eugenics Review*, 54 (1962), 143–62.

Bluhm, A., 'Eugenics and Obstetrics', in *Problems in Eugenics: Papers Communicated to the First International Eugenics Conference Held at the University of London, July 24–30, 1912*, vol. I, London 1912, 387–95.

Bock, G., 'Racism and Sexism in Nazi Germany: Motherhood, Compulsory Sterilization and the State', in R. Bridenthal, A. Grossman and M. Kaplan, eds, *When Biology Became Destiny: Women in Weimar and Nazi Germany*, New York 1984, 271–96.

Bock, G. and Thane, P., eds, *Maternity and Gender Policies: Women and the Rise of the European Welfare States, 1880s–1950s*, London and New York, 1991, 1–20.

Bracher, K. D., *The German Dictatorship: The Origins, Structure and Effects of National Socialism*, New York 1970. Translation by J. Steinberg.

Breitman, R., *The Architect of Genocide: Himmler and the Final Solution*, New York 1991.

Broszat, M., 'Hitler and the Genesis of the 'Final Solution': An Assessment of David Irving's Thesis', *Yad Vashem Studies*, 13 (1979), 73–125.

—— *The Hitler State: The Foundation and Development of the Internal Structure of the Third Reich*, New York and London 1981. Translation by J. W. Hidden.

Browning, C. R., *The Path to Genocide: Essays on Launching the Final Solution*, Cambridge, England 1992.

Bullock, A., *Hitler: A Study in Tyranny*, London 1952.

Burleigh, M., *Death and Deliverance: 'Euthanasia' in Germany, c. 1900–45*, Cambridge 1994.

Burleigh, M. and Wipperman, W., *The Racial State: Germany, 1933–1945*, Cambridge 1991.

Chase, A., *The Legacy of Malthus: The Social Costs of the New Scientific Racism*, Urbana, Illinois 1980.

Dahrendorf, R., *Society and Democracy in Germany*, New York and London 1979.

David, H. P., Fleischhacker, J. and Höhn, C., 'Abortion and Eugenics in Nazi Germany', *Population and Development Review*, 14 (1988), 81–112.

Dawidowicz, L., *The War Against the Jews*, New York 1975.

Duster, T., *Backdoor to Eugenics*, New York and London 1990.

Feldman, G. D., *Army, Industry and Labor in Germany, 1914–18*, Princeton, New Jersey 1966.

Fleming, G., *Hitler and the Final Solution*, Oxford 1986.

Folsom, J. K., *The Family and Democratic Society*, New York and London 1934.

Giannella, D., 'Eugenic Sterilization and the Law', in J. Robitscher, ed., *Eugenic Sterilizations*, Springfield, Illinois 1973.

Hauner, M. L., 'A German Racial Revolution?', *Journal of Contemporary History*, 19 (1984), 669–87.

Hilberg, R., *The Destruction of the European Jews*, Second Edition, New York 1983.

Hitler, A., *Mein Kampf*, London 1969. Introduction by D. C. Watt.

Hofer, W., 'Fifty Years On: Historians and the Third Reich', *Journal of Contemporary History*, 21 (1986), 225–51.

Irving, D., *Hitler's War*, London 1977.

Jones, G., *Social Hygiene in Twentieth Century Britain*, London 1986.

Kershaw, I., *The Nazi Dictatorship: Problems and Perspectives of Interpretation*, London 1985.

Kirkpatrick, C., *Nazi Germany: Its Women and Family Life*, New York and Indianapolis 1938.

Koonz, C., *Mothers in the Fatherland: Women, the Family and Nazi Politics*, London 1987.

Kudlien, F., 'The German Response to the Birth-rate Problem during the Third Reich', *Continuity and Change*, 5 (1990), 225–47.

Landman, J. H., *Human Sterilization: The History of the Sexual Sterilization Movement*, New York 1932.

Lerner, R., *Final Solutions: Biology, Prejudice and Genocide*, Philadelphia, Pennsylvania 1992.

Lifton, R. J., *The Nazi Doctors: Medical Killing and the Psychology of Genocide*, New York 1986.

Ludmerer, K. M., *Genetics and American Society: A Historical Appraisal*, Baltimore, Maryland 1972.

Macnicol, J., 'Eugenics and the Campaign for Voluntary Sterilization in Britain Between the Wars', *Social History of Medicine*, 2 (1989), 147–71.

Marrus, M. R., *The Holocaust in History*, London 1988.

Marrus, M. R. and Paxton, R. O., *Vichy France and the Jews*, New York 1981.

Mason, T., 'The Primacy of Politics-Politics and Economics in National Socialist Germany', in S. J. Woolf, ed., *The Nature of Fascism*, London 1968, 165–96.

Melching, W., ' "A New Morality": Left-wing Intellectuals on Sexuality in Weimar Germany', *Journal of Contemporary History*, 25 (1990), 69–85.

Michaelis, M., *Mussolini and the Jews: German–Italian Relations and the Jewish Question, 1922–1945*, Oxford 1978.

Mommsen, H., 'National Socialism: Continuity and Change', in W. Lacqueur, ed., *Fascism: A Reader's Guide*, Cambridge, England 1976, 179–210.

Mosse, G.L., *The Crisis of German Ideology: Intellectual Origins of the Third Reich*, New York 1964.

—— *Toward the Final Solution. A History of European Racism*, New York and London 1978.

Müller-Hill, B., *Murderous Science: Elimination by Scientific Selection of*

Jews, Gypsies and Others: Germany 1933–1945, Oxford 1988. Translation by G. R. Fraser.

Noakes, J. 'Nazism and Eugenics: the Background to the Nazi Sterilization Law of 14 July 1933', in B. J. Bullen, H. Pogge Von Strandmann and A. B. Polonsky, eds, *Ideas into Politics*, London 1984, 75–94.

Noakes, J. and Pridham, G., *Nazism, 1919–1945*, vol. 2, *State, Economy and Society, 1933–1939*, Exeter 1984; vol. 3, *Foreign Policy, War and Racial Extermination*, Exeter 1988.

Paul, J., 'State Eugenic Sterilization History: A Brief Overview', in J. Robitscher, ed., *Eugenic Sterilization*, Springfield, Illinois 1973, 20–31.

Poliakov, L., *The Aryan Myth: A History of Racist and Nationalist Ideas in Europe*, New York 1977. Translation by E. Howard.

Preti, L., 'Fascist Imperialism and Racism', in R. Sarti ed., *The Ax Within: Italian Fascism in Action*, New York 1974, 187–207.

Proctor, R.N., *Racial Hygiene. Medicine under the Nazis*, Cambridge, Massachusetts and London 1988.

Reilly, P., *Genetics, Law, and Social Policy*, Cambridge, Massachusetts and London 1977.

Robertson, E. M., 'Race as a Factor in Mussolini's Policy in Africa and Europe', *Journal of Contemporary History*, 23 (1988), 37–58.

Sauer, W., 'National Socialism: Totalitarianism or Fascism?', *American Historical Review*, LXXIII (1967), 404–24.

Seidal, G., *The Holocaust Denial*, Leeds 1986.

Soloway, R. A., *Demography and Degeneration: Eugenics and the Declining Birthrate in Twentieth-Century Britain*, Chapel Hill, North Carolina 1990.

Stephenson, J., ' "Reichsbund der Kinderreichen": the League of Large Families in the Population Policy of Nazi Germany', *European Studies Review*, 9 (1979), 350–75.

Stern, F., *The Politics of Cultural Despair: A Study in the Rise of the Germanic Ideology*, Berkeley 1961.

Stille, A., *Benevolence and Betrayal: Five Italian Jewish Families under Fascism*, London 1988.

Stoehr, I., 'Housework and Motherhood: Debates and Policies in the Women's Movement in Imperial Germany and the Weimar Republic', in G. Bock and P. Thane, eds, *Maternity and Gender Policies: Women and the Rise of the European Welfare States, 1880s–1950s*, London and New York 1991, 213–32.

Taylor Allen, A., 'Mothers of the New Generation: Adele Schreiber, Helene Stöcker, and the Evolution of a German Idea of Motherhood, 1900–1914', *Signs*, 10 (1985), 418–38.

Thane, P., *The Foundations of the Welfare State*, London and New York 1982.

Usborne, C., 'Abortion in Weimar Germany – the Debate among the Medical Profession', *Continuity and Change*, 5 (1990), 199–224.

—— ' "Pregnancy is the Woman's Active Service": Pronatalism in Germany during the First World War', in R. Wall and J. Winter, eds, *The Upheaval of War: Family, Work and Welfare in Europe, 1914–1918*, Cambridge, England and New York 1988, 389–416.

Van Wagenen, B., 'Report on Sterilization in the United States', in C. Rosenberg, ed., *Problems in Eugenics: First International Eugenics Con-*

ference, 1912, Held at the University of London, July 24–30, 1912, New York and London 1984, 365–70.

Webster, P., *Pétain's Crime: The Full Story of French Collaboration in the Holocaust*, London 1990.

Weindling, P., *Darwinism and Social Darwinism in Imperial Germany: The Contribution of the Cell Biologist Oscar Hertwig (1849–1922)*, Stuttgart and New York 1991.

—— *Health, Race, and German Politics between National Unification and Nazism, 1870–1945*, Cambridge, England 1989.

—— 'The Medical Profession, Social Hygiene and the Birth Rate in Germany, 1914–18', in R. Wall and J. Winter, eds., *The Upheaval of War: Family, Work and Welfare in Europe, 1914–1918*, Cambridge, England and New York 1988, 417–38.

Weiss, S. F., 'The Race Hygiene Movement in Germany, 1904–1945', in M. B. Adams, ed., *The Wellborn Science: Eugenics in Germany, France, Brazil, and Russia*, Oxford 1990, 8–68.

Woycke, J., *Birth Control in Germany, 1871–1933*, New York 1988.

4 CONCLUSION: THE POLITICS OF RACE AND POPULATION IN THE TWENTIETH CENTURY

Baldwin, P., *The Politics of Social Solidarity: Class Bases of the European Welfare State, 1875–1975*, Cambridge and New York 1990.

Bruce, M., *The Coming of the Welfare State*, London 1972.

Chamberlin, J. E. and Gilman, S. L., eds, *Degeneration: The Dark Side of Progress*, New York 1985.

Eagle Russett, C., *Sexual Science: The Victorian Construction of Womanhood*, Cambridge, Massachusetts 1989.

Marshall, T. H., *Class, Citizenship and Social Development*, Chicago 1963.

Nead, L., *Myths of Sexuality: Representations of Women in Victorian Britain*, Oxford 1988.

Pick, D., *Faces of Degeneration: A European Disorder, c. 1848–1918*, Cambridge 1989.

Showalter, E., *The Female Malady: Women, Madness and English Culture, 1830–1980*, London 1987.

Swaan, A. de, *In Care of the State: Health Care, Education and Welfare in Europe in the Modern Era*, Oxford 1988.

Weindling, P., 'Compulsory Sterilisation in National Socialist Germany', *German History*, 5 (1987), 10–24.

Other sources

Bacci, M. L. *A History of Italian Fertility During the Last Two Centuries*, New York 1974.

Blacker, C. P., *Eugenics: Galton and After*, London 1952.

Caldwell, L., 'Reproducers of the Nation: Women and the Family in Fascist Policy', in D. Forgacs, ed., *Rethinking Italian Fascism: Capitalism, Populism and Culture*, London 1986, 110–41.

Douglass, W. A., 'The Southern Italian Family: A Critique', *Journal of Family History*, 5 (1980), 338–59.

Dupâquier, J., ed., *Histoire de la Population Française*, vol. 4, Paris 1988.

Dyer, C., *Population and Society in Twentieth-Century France*, London 1978.

Evans, R. J. and Lee, W. E., eds, *The German Family*, London 1981.

Eversley, D. E. C., *Social Theories of Fertility and the Malthusian Debate*, Oxford 1959.

Foucault, M., *The History of Sexuality*, New York 1978.

Freeden, M., 'Eugenics and Ideology', *Historical Journal*, 26 (1983), 959–62.

—— 'Eugenics and Progressive Thought: A Study in Ideological Affinity', *The Historical Journal*, 22 (1979), 645–71.

Gasman, D., *The Scientific Origins of National Socialism*, New York 1972.

Glass, D. V., ed., *Introduction to Malthus*, London 1953.

Glass, D. V. and Eversley, D. E. C., eds, *Population in History*, London 1965.

Gordon, L., 'The Politics of Population: Birth Control and the Eugenics Movement', *Radical America*, 8 (1974), 61–97.

Graham, L. R., 'Science and Values: The Eugenics Movement in Germany and Russia in the 1920s', *American Historical Review*, 82 (1977), 1133–64.

Hale, O. J., 'Adolf Hitler and the Post-War German Birthrate', *Journal of Central European Affairs*, XVIII (1957), 166–73.

Hiorns, R. W., ed., *Demographic Patterns in Developed Societies*, London 1980.

Jones, G., 'Eugenics and Social Policy Between the Wars', *The Historical Journal*, 25 (1982), 717–28.

Kater, M. H., *Doctors under Hitler: The German Medical Profession in Crisis During the Third Reich*, Chapel Hill, North Carolina 1989.

Kirk, M., Bacci, M. L., and Szabady, E., eds, *Law and Fertility in Europe*, Dolhain 1975.

Knodel, J. E., *The Decline of Fertility in Germany, 1871–1939*, Princeton, New Jersey 1974.

Leadbetter, R., *History of the Malthusian League, 1877–1927*, Colombus, Ohio 1976.

Morel, B. A., *Traité des Dégénérescences*, Paris 1857.

Nordau, M., *Degeneration*, New York 1968. Introduction by G. Mosse. (The first German edition came out in two volumes in 1893.)

Offen, K., 'Depopulation, Natalism and Feminism', *American Historical Review*, 89 (1984), 653–71.

Pickens, D. K., 'The Sterilization Movement: The Search for Purity in Mind and State', *Phylon*, 28 (1967), 78–94.

Searle, G. R., *Eugenics and Politics in Britain, 1900–1914*, Leyden 1976.

Soloway, R. A., *Birth Control and the Population Question in England, 1877–1930*, Chapel Hill, North Carolina 1982.

—— 'Counting the Degenerates: The Statistics of Race Degeneration in Edwardian England', *Journal of Contemporary History*, 17 (1982), 137–64.

Spengler, J. J., 'French Population Theory Since 1800', *Journal of Political Economy*, 44 (1936), 577–611.

Stephensen, J. *The Nazi Organisation of Women*, London 1981.

—— *Women in Nazi Society*, London 1975.

Swart, K. W., *The Sense of Decadence in Nineteenth Century France*, The Hague 1965.

Teitelbaum, M. S. and Winter, J. M., *The Fear of Population Decline*, San Diego, California 1985.

Weindling, P., 'Fascism and Population Policies in Comparative European Perspective', *Population and Development Review*, supplement to volume 14 (1989), 102–21.

—— 'German–Soviet Co-Operation in Science: The Case of the Laboratory for Racial Research, 1931–1938', *Nuncius*, 1 (1987), 103–9.

—— 'Medicine and Modernisation', *History of Science*, 24 (1986), 277–301.

—— 'Weimar Eugenics: The Kaiser Wilhelm Institute for Anthropology, Human Heredity and Eugenics in Social Context', *Annals of Science*, 42 (1985), 303–18.

Weiss, S., *Race Hygiene and National Efficiency*, Berkeley and London 1988.

Index

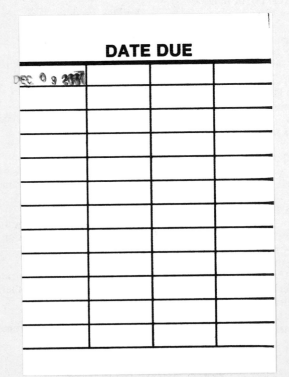

DATE DUE

DEC 0 9 2000